"In this timely writing, biblical scholar James McGrath calls us to move beyond the kind of shallow religion we often see around us and go deeper into what a loving, liberating, life-giving faith can actually be. In ways that will both make you think and make you smile, McGrath challenges us to discover anew what it means to be followers of Jesus and his way of love, transforming both our own lives and the world around us."

—**MICHAEL B. CURRY**, 27th presiding bishop of the Episcopal Church, author of *Love Is the Way: Holding on to Hope in Troubled Times*

"For all of us who have found ourselves sitting in the rubble of our once-certain faith, wondering what in the world to do next, James F. McGrath has helpful ideas. Advising against giving up in despair or rushing to new certainties and fundamentalisms, he invites us to inhabit a faith that works, explores, experiences, and connects. I found this book to be generous, compassionate, and wise. I believe it will be a good companion for all of us interested in rebuilding our faith on the other side of deconstruction."

—**SARAH BESSEY**, author of *Field Notes for the Wilderness: Practices for an Evolving Faith*

"*Beyond Deconstruction* is a pastoral and practical, commonsensical and compassionate guide to faith reconstruction for post-evangelicals and post-fundamentalists. A significant contribution to the religious landscape!"

—**DAVID P. GUSHEE**, author of *After Evangelicalism: The Path to a New Christianity*

"James McGrath has accomplished something remarkable: he's shown us how to be more biblical by being less biblicist, more Christian by being less dogmatic, and more faithful by embracing uncertainty. *Beyond Deconstruction* is simultaneously a demolition manual for toxic faith and a construction guide for something far better. With the wisdom of a seasoned biblical scholar and the heart of a compassionate mentor, he offers a road map for those who refuse to choose between intellectual honesty and spiritual depth. This isn't just deconstruction; it's resurrection. McGrath shows us how the ruins of collapsed certainty can become the foundation stones for a faith that is both more humble and more beautiful than before. McGrath's fourfold framework—faith that works, explores, experiences, and connects—provides a holistic vision for a faith that doesn't discard its blessings when moving beyond the burdens of certainty."

—**TRIPP FULLER**, host of *Homebrewed Christianity* podcast

BEYOND DECONSTRUCTION

BUILDING A MORE EXPANSIVE FAITH

JAMES F. McGRATH

WILLIAM B. EERDMANS PUBLISHING COMPANY
GRAND RAPIDS, MICHIGAN

Wm. B. Eerdmans Publishing Co.
2006 44th Street SE, Grand Rapids, MI 49508
www.eerdmans.com

Published 2026
Printed in the United States of America

32 31 30 29 28 27 26 1 2 3 4 5 6 7

ISBN 978-0-8028-8459-6

Library of Congress Cataloging-in-Publication Data

A catalog record for this book is available from the Library of Congress.

Unless otherwise noted, Scripture quotations are from the New Revised Standard Version, updated edition.

Contents

INTRODUCTION

Faith That Collapses
(and What to Do Next)

There is a lot of talk at the moment about "deconstruction." Deconstruction in the popular sense refers to taking apart your belief system.* What the term doesn't capture is that for so many people the process is not the meticulous disassembly of a LEGO fortress, each piece going back in the box to be enjoyed on another occasion. Often the label "destruction" feels more apt than "deconstruction." It is the terrifying collapse of a worldview that you had been inhabiting. If it weren't trademarked, perhaps people would be talking about the Jengafication of their faith rather than deconstruction. What often happens is that blocks are identified that can no longer remain comfortably and so need to be removed. That sounds more like what the word "deconstruction" describes—until that moment when the tower comes crashing down. The key question people of faith ask in the aftermath is whether, as would be the case with Jenga, this means you've lost the game. The answer is emphatically no, but I realize that can be cold comfort when your cherished beliefs are lying in an irreparable pile on the floor.

This book is less about the process of deconstruction in itself than about what happens next. Deconstruction in the most dramatic cases looks a lot like destruction, but even in the wake of

* For someone working at a university, the first thing that comes to mind when we hear that term is an approach to literature pioneered by Jacques Derrida. That is most definitely *not* what the current conversation is about, and not what this book is about.

total destruction there remains the hope that that end is not final, that something else and even something better may lie in the future. This book is intended first and foremost for those who have foreseen that the process of building something new in place of their collapsed worldview will be a DIY project. Hopefully saying that will not give the wrong impression. I wrote those words very intentionally as someone who has done a variety of floor, electrical, plumbing, lawnmower, and other repairs only because others have shared their expertise. Those who know me know that I'm most certainly not a handyman. I am, however, good at finding answers to questions and following instructions, which means that I can fix things nonetheless. Whether you are trying to repair something or learn a song, and whether you turn first to books or YouTube videos, the underlying principle is the same. Being "self-taught" or pursuing a DIY project doesn't mean you have to reinvent the wheel on your own, or that you have no one to thank but yourself. It means taking responsibility for the work rather than outsourcing it to someone else. If untrustworthy religious authorities were part of the collapse of your previous belief system, that is likely another reason you might have a strong preference not to simply rely on someone else to do this work for you. Yet, on the other hand, it is especially important in this era in which more and more people claim to "do their own research" to emphasize what those of us who actually do research know full well: we all depend on others, and there is no possibility of this being otherwise. None of us is an expert in everything, and no one is infallible even within their own area of specialization.

After their old way of thinking stops working, many adopt another system of thought to replace it, something ready-made. There are prefabricated options galore in the marketplace of faiths. But let the buyer beware! All of them are human constructs, just like the one that let you down so spectacularly. That doesn't mean they are all the same or all equally good or bad. Some are clearly worse than others. This is just a warning and a reminder that none of them is perfect. There is no perfect house or perfect car, either, and that doesn't mean you shouldn't own one. What it means is that your expectations must be realistic if you are not to set yourself up for unnecessary disappointment. If a worldview or a vehicle works perfectly for a while, that cannot be the case forever. That's just the nature of what we build in this universe, whether physical edifices or mental constructs. Ready-made options require less effort on your part, but after disappointment with one of them, it might be time to try something tailor-made for your specifications. That will require not only effort but patience. You may therefore be tempted to simply grab for a worldview that is on offer as a package, if it does a pretty satisfying job of addressing whatever troubled you most about your previously held views, whatever the fatal flaw was that you have identified as responsible for its collapse. That is like choosing a car only because it has a great sound system, to replace the one in your previous car that was frustratingly bad. Not that you shouldn't look for something that does better than what you previously had. Don't get me wrong. I am just emphasizing that, after a disappointment, we often focus on what went wrong to the exclusion of other considerations. That car with the expensive subwoofers might also let in a lot of road noise, not to mention that it lacks a rear windshield wiper. When you are too focused on what was wrong with the old car, or house, or faith, you are prone to overlook other things, or to let them slide, confident that you'll learn to live with them. And initially you're downright happy. Yet, pretty soon it will become clear that the vehicle or the faith you've bought has strengths and weaknesses, just like your previous one. It may have different and perhaps even opposite strengths and weaknesses, making it initially appealing, but eventually its shortcomings become an issue. This is why, after a big disappointment, you don't want to jump quickly to a rebound worldview. Only you can decide whether you've moved far enough through and beyond the process of deconstruction and the painful loss that accompanied it to be ready for something new. Even after some time passes, you'll still come with baggage. That's okay—so will your new worldview.

Suggesting that you not look for a "prefab faith" in the marketplace of ideas does not mean you should try to create something completely new from scratch. Even if you wanted to, you couldn't. Just as a new house will not be entirely unlike any other home that has ever been built, no newly invented religion has ever managed to be entirely unlike anything that ever existed before. Even trying to make something the opposite of something else is a form of influence, and it is possible to hold diametrically opposed beliefs and yet to approach them in much the same way. An atheist in the United States may think they have abandoned the Christianity of their upbringing, while someone from another culture or tradition may see more clearly how that individual still retains much of their prior way of thinking. Sometimes those who "deconvert" substitute denial of fundamentalist Christian dogmas for affirmation thereof, without even taking a close look at the underlying framework: they simply become antireligious fundamentalists that are a mirror image of what they once were. Although my answer to the question "Why are you still a Christian?" includes many facets, one is that I am aware that I am so steeped in that tradition through a combination of culture, upbringing, and personal experience that any attempt to pretend I was departing from it would risk being dishonest about how deeply Christian influences run.

Hopefully this last point makes clear that, in recommending that you not get something ready-made, I am in no sense suggesting that your new system cannot be a different form of the broad tradition you previously inhabited. Indeed, often one of the most exciting parts of reconstruction is discovering a previously unknown breadth to a tradition that you experienced as narrow, and knew only a sliver of. Those deeper historical and wider contemporary expressions of your religion become resources in the rebuilding project, whatever precisely you set out to build, and regardless whether the end result resembles the blueprint you had in mind early in the process. The point of the DIY metaphor is for you to take responsibility for the building, and for choosing precisely what the details of the new structure will look like. You may be tempted to replace your old faith either with one that is as close to identical to it as possible or one that resembles it as little as possible. Instead, I recommend making small, specific choices about the individual elements rather than a vast, sweeping decision about the whole. If something seems to be largely what you are looking for, still be prepared to customize.

A major assumption in all this is that you *want* to build something new in place of what you had. It is possible to become comfortable living on the heap of rubble, emphatically telling everyone that they are living in perilous structures that are prone to collapse, while the bricks and paneling that now lie strewn beneath your feet can no longer do any comparable harm to you. When a worldview collapses, the person living in it gets injured in all sorts of ways. If you rebuild, you do so in full recognition that there are risks and dangers. Living without a shelter is not risk-free either. If you have genuinely learned to be happier without some of the deceptive comforts of your old home, there are probably other things that you miss. You may be scared of being hurt again in another collapse. This book seeks to combine realism about that as a prospect with guidance for how to courageously build despite the risk, and to do so wisely so as to minimize the chance of having a similar experience again. Going forward, you will be prepared to perform periodic maintenance and upgrades on your worldview. If you try to keep a car or house the way it was built with no changes, it eventually wears out catastrophically. This book will help you transition to viewing your worldview as something dynamic that not only can change but is *supposed to* grow, develop, and improve with time. Even though religions sometimes claim to be unchanging, anyone who studies their history can show you that's a lie. The very effort to maintain the façade of permanence and unshakability stood in the way of letting your faith be something vibrant and living. This book aims to help you avoid making that mistake again.

If the only reason you haven't rebuilt is the resentment you're harboring against the dishonest realtor or builder who sold you the last one that now lies in a heap, that in itself is a reason to build anew. Living in resentment is understandable as an immediate response to what happened, but it is not advisable in the long term. If you continue to suffer and do without good things because of that experience, you are allowing those who harmed you to continue to do so. Even if what you build is not something you inhabit permanently, it may be a crucial next step in moving on. Let that be enough for now. You held cherished beliefs and they let you down. It is not only fine but necessary to rebuild with an awareness that, while your aim is for it to be *durable,* no human construction can be *permanent.* If you were sold a structure that turned out to be structurally unsound, with a sinking foundation and no hope for preservation or restoration, you have a right to feel cheated, jaded, and skeptical. That isn't a reason to remain homeless if there are other options available. People live in homes and people inhabit worldviews. I want, in this book, to help you move beyond the hurt of your past experiences and into freedom and healing. The truth is that you've inevitably already been shaping a new worldview. No one is without one. Yet its contours may be defined mostly or entirely in terms of what it is not. Your core values likewise may be simple negations of your old ones. This book seeks to help you formulate your stance and outlook in positive terms. Not just "I no longer believe X" or "I'm not a Y" but "here is what I believe, what I stand for, what I value, and what I hope for."

It is important to know that what you build does not need to function in the same way as the system it replaces did. To explore our building analogy further, imagine a literal church building that has collapsed. A classic, historic stone church building complete with steeple and monodirectionally oriented pews is now a ruin of rocks, mortar, splinters, and shards of stained glass. Those who previously used the building might try to replicate the original as closely as possible. They might opt for a more contemporary appearance but plan to resume traditional worship services of the sort they were familiar with. They might not even consider other possibilities, but they should. What if, instead of a building optimized for pulpit preaching, they set up a place that encourages conversation? That might be an open hall, a coffee shop, a pub, or something else. It might be a place where delivering a traditional sermon would be a challenge. As we explore later in this book, one person with authority proclaiming their message to everyone else was once the only way to disseminate information. Today that is no longer the case, and what once was the optimal means to accomplish something may actually hinder accomplishing it now. There are often multiple means of facilitating the same kind of aims and a similar experience, not all of which will work equally well for all individuals and groups in all contexts. The same community that once focused on singing and listening to sermons in that location may develop a vision to emphasize other things. What if they build a school or a hospital with a chapel, rather than a traditional church building, because they decide that worship to the exclusion of all else was the wrong focus? When your convictions and values change, the places you gather and the worldview you embrace should be set up to reflect and facilitate that shift in focus.

One of the central themes that runs through this book is that, in most cases, what you have experienced is the collapse of a belief system in the strict sense of that phrase: a set of doctrines that you were taught you must subscribe to, which unraveled and came apart. In talking about rebuilding your *faith*, I am not referring to putting new dogmas in place of the old ones. When I worked through this process, I discovered that my faith is something deeper, broader, and fundamentally different from that narrow definition. The question is not whether you will have beliefs. Everyone does. The question is whether assent to doctrinal propositions is going to provide the foundation for your new construction. If you can't imagine anything else as a possibility, and quite literally have no idea what I am talking about, just hold on. You're going to enjoy this book immensely, wherever your own journey of faith ultimately takes you. I'm going to take you on a trip to some places it sounds like you've never been. Looking at lots of examples of what others have done is a natural and arguably a necessary part of the rebuilding process, not because you need to emulate what others have done (although you are obviously free to do that) but because the more examples you see of what is possible, the more ideas you will have for what you can do, what your options are. You'll come up with new ideas that are not exactly like any ideas you have seen before, even if not entirely unlike them. You'll also try to actively avoid some of the things that you've seen, because you've investigated them and discovered they are not for you. Often those who've been steeped in a fundamentalist mind-set have approached all contact with those who are different as a battle that must be won. I invite you to approach the different ways of being a religious person or community as opportunities to learn, to consider other models, and to take responsibility for accepting and emulating, for rejecting and avoiding, or for adapting.

Why Me?

Why should a New Testament professor write a book on building something new after deconstruction? There are a couple of reasons, one of which motivated me to write this book, but another didn't fully occur to me until I started working on it. Many academics (myself included) pursued the study of the Bible because of a personal faith shaped by some form of conservative religious belief. Studying the Bible with (initially strange and unfamiliar) academic tools, and being exposed to a wide array of arguments and conclusions from other perspectives, is something we may initially resist. Eventually, however, it becomes clear that the Bible is not what we assumed it to be. For me the turning point in rejecting the idea that the Bible was inerrant was recognizing that I was actually defending that doctrine *about* the Bible from evidence within the Bible itself. That meant that (in practice if not in theory) the doctrine of inerrancy was functioning as my ultimate authority, and the Bible was not allowed to overrule it. Since the very point of affirming inerrancy was supposed to be upholding the authority of the Bible, it didn't take long to realize this was self-defeating. While deconstruction is being experienced much more widely in the present day, it mirrors an experience that academics in biblical studies have had for generations. This means that people like myself have been pioneers. We went down the road you are traveling ahead of you, and we can share what we have learned from the journey.

If studying the Bible academically often triggers deconstruction, that means not only that people like me have experienced it ourselves, but also that our academic publications may have been responsible for someone else experiencing it. If it wasn't me in your case, then it may have been a different New Testament scholar. That being so, it seems that in addition to having experience that we *can* share, we actually have a *responsibility* to share what we have learned along the way. Academics of course share what they have learned about their subject matter, but that doesn't address how studying the Bible impacted us personally. There have been a handful of personal narratives from scholars about loss of faith, clinging to faith, or experiencing a new and exciting faith as a result of the academic study of the Bible.* These have been helpful to me, and I am sure they are to others. As far as I am aware, however, none of them offers what I am offering here, that is, a *guide* to and reflection on the process itself. To that end, the book takes into account what others have experienced and learned along the way, as well as my own insights and perspectives. One individual traveler's perspective can be useful if you want to follow the same route they did. A map app (shouldn't we just call that a mapp?) will provide what you need if you happen to already know where you want to go. Guidebooks for tourists have a different aim: to provide recommendations and give you options for different routes you can travel and different things you can see and do along the way.

In the remainder of this introduction, I'll share a few details from my own experience of the early stages of exploration and reconstruction. From there I'll survey a range of options for things that your faith may come to focus on in whole or in part. In most instances there will be room for all of them even if they are not all equally central. You might think of them (to return once again to our metaphor of building) as individual rooms or wings in a multipurpose structure you construct. Let me say once more that there's no need to put something *permanent* in place. While the loss of something that seemed permanent was almost inevitably traumatic for you,

* See, for instance, the collection edited by John Byron and Joel N. Lohr, *I (Still) Believe: Leading Bible Scholars Share Their Stories of Faith and Scholarship* (Grand Rapids: Zondervan, 2015).

what hurt more than the falling beliefs was the loss of a *feeling* of certainty, of stability, of safety that you had because of that structure's illusion of permanence. In order to move on, it is crucial to look back and take stock, and to recognize honestly that the biggest issue with your prior belief system was not any individual belief so much as the way others made those beliefs seem God-given, set in stone for all time, a house built upon the rock that could never be shaken. Since it is a biblical image that is often misused and misunderstood, and it resonates with the theme of this book, we will return to the image of the house built upon the rock in the next chapter.

A religious faith is just one component in human culture. The culture in any society in any part of the world seems natural, given, the obvious way of doing things to anyone who lives within it, at least if it is all they've experienced. If you leave your home country and spend time elsewhere, you undergo culture shock, a process of frustration by difference, followed by recognition that at least one very different way of being human works just as well as what you grew up with. You can go back to your home culture, but you're never the same again. That is often uncomfortable, sometimes more so than adjusting to another culture was, leading people to refer to it as "reverse culture shock." This is not an argument against travel. On the contrary, I'm an advocate for spending enough time in another part of the world to have this experience, because it teaches you things that you simply cannot learn any other way. Let's be honest: most things that are worthwhile are uncomfortable. Even the common human experience of maturing into adulthood involves the trading of seeming simplicity for unnerving complexity, an illusion of safety for responsibility. If you prefer that analogy, feel free to cross out the title on the cover and rename this book *Adulting Your Faith*. Even if we sometimes reminisce nostalgically on childhood innocence when things seemed simpler, few of us would trade the satisfaction of adult struggles in the realm of family, career, or hobby for that sense of innocence and security. If more people could be convinced that what religious and cultural systems offer is an illusion, a feeling of certainty about things it is impossible to actually *be* certain of, our society would be in much better shape than it is now.

On the other hand, when people are not given the resources to cope with the responsibility of adulthood, it shouldn't be a surprise that they cling to immaturity. Hence, another reason for writing this book is the conviction that there are beautiful possibilities for you to build and explore, and that it would be tragic if you and others who've had traumatic experiences of deconstruction flee for refuge to other dogmatic systems that promise false certainty. I hope my book prevents at least some people from simply trading their old idol for a new one, robbing them in the process of something wonderful and worthwhile that could have been theirs if they had been provided enough support to make the challenging journey into a more honest, open, accurate, rich, and rewarding kind of faith.

I think the first germ of the idea for a book along these lines (which at that point I would have given the title of *Renovating Your Faith*) occurred to me precisely when you might expect it would: when we remodeled our bathroom. As first-time homeowners in a fifty-year-old house, we had a sense of what the house was like, but we had also come to expect surprises. When it seemed time to improve the bathroom, replacing the tiles on the floor was an obvious thing to do. What the crew of workers soon unveiled was something that neither we nor they could have foreseen. Beneath the visible tiles there was another layer of tiles, and then underneath that, a layer of linoleum, and only under that the flooring, which was not in the best of shape. It was clear what needed to be done. Tear it all out and replace it. Before I knew it, peering through the door to the bathroom gave me an unprecedented view of the crawl space beneath the house. There is a metaphor here that may be useful. It is not surprising that *What Lies Beneath* seemed a fitting title for a horror movie. Even though I have never seen the film, the phrase jumped into my mind when I peered down past where the familiar floor had been. Since then we've had a new roof built, during which someone's misplaced step resulted in a leg coming through the ceiling. On an earlier occasion we discovered that we really needed a new patio door because a thief tried to get in the old one, on which the latch was looser than it was supposed to be. I won't elaborate on those stories since I want my family to be able to read this book without being traumatized too much. The point is this: one's home is, more than anyplace else, a place in which one seeks the illusion of safety. In most instances, the house does provide some safety from thieves and from the elements. Yet all it takes is a hailstorm, and you discover that the roof that keeps the rain off your head is not a perfect defense. Yes, that happened to us too.

These kinds of experiences would lead some to look for another house, or tear the current one down completely and build a new one. In my case, they made me eager to stay and work to improve the structure I was inhabiting. Here I was becoming increasingly aware of the flaws, the shortcomings, and could address them. In a new house, whether brand-new or previously owned, everything would look pristine and in good repair. But there, too, surprises would lurk beneath the surface. They might be minor or major, and they might matter a little to you or matter a lot. But you could never live there without having to perform maintenance and repairs, and whether those problems would be fewer and less significant or more numerous and far worse than in your current house is impossible to tell in advance. This is another significant part of my answer when someone asks me, "Why (and in what sense) are you still a Christian?" Trading my current system for a different one might address some of the issues in the one I currently have, but it would come with other issues. I've chosen to work on making my home and my faith ones that I am happy to dwell in, enjoying what is nice, fixing what I can, and reminding myself that nothing is perfect when that's all I can do. I wouldn't be surprised if the famous serenity prayer was first uttered specifically about the person's house. It seems to apply equally well to faith. We might reword it ever so slightly to "God, grant me the serenity to accept the things I cannot fix, the courage to fix the things I can, and the wisdom to know the difference."

Carl Sagan made an analogy between buying a used car and choosing a religion.* Even if your faith-construction project is DIY, akin to building your own car rather than buying one ready-made, the analogy still stands. Either way, you cannot safely jump from "I need one of these" to clicking buy on something that sounds like it might be exactly what you're looking for. Caution is needed for countless reasons. The product might be top of the line, authentic, but not the right fit for the rest of your configuration. It might be a good fit but a cheap knock-off. If you're shopping for a car and don't know cars, you should bring someone along who does. Have you ever noticed how rarely those shopping for a faith actually consult an expert on the subject? How might "church shopping" be different if you could bring along a theologian or a biblical scholar? Anyway, I'll be the first to admit that isn't always possible, and to be honest, might not always be in your best interest. We biblical scholars who listen to sermons are far more fussy than you probably are and are liable to quibble about minute details. When you're shopping for a car, you need someone who can spot major problems; you don't need someone who will be overly fussy about which brand of spark plugs is the best. Anyway, more often than

* Carl Sagan, *The Varieties of Scientific Experience* (New York: Penguin Books, 2006), 144–45.

not you go shopping without an expert to help you. What do you do? Just arm yourself with a healthy dose of skepticism. Don't simply believe the salesperson when they say the car was only driven once by a little old lady, or that they can't go lower on the price. Either claim might in fact be true—the point is, you cannot just take it on trust that it is. You need to dare to question, to investigate, to challenge.

That doesn't mean being cynical. For those old enough to remember the show, the slogan from the *X-Files*, "Trust No One," is impossible. We see that all too clearly in the show's protagonist, Fox Mulder. He distrusts official government claims but trusts all kinds of people who claim to know what's really going on behind the scenes. This leaves him open to manipulation in ways that are at least as bad as, and perhaps worse than, the everyday manipulation of the public that governments and advertisers are prone to engage in. In short, if you think that an existing worldview will work for you, before you buy it, take a look under the hood. My point about DIY is not that you won't find a basic model that you can work with. On the contrary, there is no real way to invent a worldview that is completely different from what someone has already come up with. The point is to be prepared to fix and to customize.

My own experience didn't involve a catastrophic collapse of my worldview when I studied the Bible, but a consistent if at times halting evolution, one in which I often clung to an older way of thinking about things for longer than I had any reason to. Sometimes that was because I personally thought I was supposed to; sometimes it was because I was working somewhere that explicitly said I must hold certain views. Teaching for the past couple of decades at a university that does not have a religious affiliation definitely helped save my faith, allowing it to continue to evolve rather than be smothered to death by constraints on what I was permitted to say and explore. It shouldn't be surprising that a secular context would be conducive to my faith journey. An environment that neither imposes a faith nor is hostile to yours allows you the freedom to explore and grow, to change your mind and perhaps change it back again. While parents often send their children to sectarian schools hoping to keep them isolated from worldly influences, often they are simply setting them up for a bigger crisis of faith when they get into the working world. Often the result is loss of faith rather than growth and change. Fundamentalism is incredibly fragile and needs to be isolated from threats. That should tell you something about its claims to be sturdy. Somehow this seems obvious looking at it from the outside. Sometimes the collapse of its house of cards involves self-fulfilling prophecies you are liable to hear in sermons. For instance, I've heard preachers say that if the Bible isn't 100 percent the Word of God, then you might as well throw it in the trash. That message is as illogical as it is dangerous. On the one hand, one's parents are not infallible, yet that doesn't mean it is wise to ignore them. They may not always be right, but that doesn't mean they are mostly wrong. If the Bible is a collection of human texts written by people who had profound spiritual and moral insights, it is worth reading. It doesn't need to be qualitatively different from every other text to be important and useful. Rhetoric about a stark either/or is just one more example of the idolatrous search for the illusion of certainty. Conservative Christians are prone to make the Bible, the work of human hands, stand in for God, and to ascribe to it attributes of divinity such as infallibility and perfection.

I was fortunate enough to have professors and to read books by people who shared my faith yet didn't close the door on questions. Some of them even directed me away from doctrines like inerrancy or the "end times" approach to the book of Revelation. They did so not as an attack on my faith but as an expression of our shared faith, based in their own interest in my spiritual well-being. That is one reason why, although I initially resisted many academic insights and perspectives related to the Bible, I did not flee from them nor flat-out reject them. If you've had similar good fortune, you might be reading this to renovate your faith while it is still standing, to maintain its overall soundness by replacing that which no longer works. This book is not aimed at those seeking a superficial remodel; it is not a fresh coat of paint applied to something they plan to leave largely as is without even taking a close look. This book is a guide to undertaking a close inspection of one's faith, not in the interest of destroying it but in the interest of having whatever is worth keeping thrive, while identifying and replacing whatever needs to be replaced. Sometimes what needs to go is simply out of date (your contractor might say "not up to code"). But sometimes when we look behind paneling and under flooring, we find things growing that are toxic, and that can be true of faith, just as it can be of a building. Making such discoveries and doing something about the problems are crucial to the well-being of those who inhabit it and everyone else around.

Finding Your Foundation

Blogging was extremely helpful at every stage of my journey from deconstruction to reconstruction. Early on, when no one was listening, I found the courage to say things publicly that I hadn't before. Later, when I had an audience, I was able to benefit from input from a wide variety of perspectives, keeping me from merely moving out of one ideological bubble into another of the same sort. I will never forget (and still use in my own teaching) a thought experiment that an atheist commenter on my blog presented to me.* They said I could have a machine that could take me anywhere

* I have shared this before in James F. McGrath, *Theology and Science Fiction* (Eugene, OR: Cascade, 2016), 48–50.

in time or space. (Basically the TARDIS from *Doctor Who*. You can see why I loved this.) I should use it with a question in mind: What would it take to make me lose my faith? The atheist's expectation was that I would realize that my beliefs were unfalsifiable, and so I'd abandon them.

If you're not familiar with the term, saying a belief is unfalsifiable means that no counterevidence could disprove that belief. If I say the moon is made of cheese, and you present me with moon rocks to show me otherwise, and my reply is that those rocks are simply a different sort of cheese, you'll immediately realize that no new evidence will dissuade me from what I assume to be true. It is easy to say that your religious worldview is rational and open to revision in light of new evidence, but a time machine might really put that to the test, depending on where and when you were willing to go with it. As I explored the thought experiment, I was surprised by what it revealed about my faith.

My first instinct was to witness the burial of Jesus, after which I could sit outside the tomb and watch to see if anything interesting happened. It soon struck me that the question of whether God vindicated Jesus beyond death was not the same as the question of what happened to his corpse. After all, couldn't God raise martyrs who were burned at the stake? If Jesus had been thrown to the dogs, would that prevent God from vindicating him?* Any such affirmation was and should be a theological claim, and could not be a historical one. I had an inkling of this already from my study

* John Dominic Crossan famously proposed that Jesus's body would indeed have been left to be devoured by dogs and other scavengers. See his *Jesus: A Revolutionary Biography* (New York: HarperCollins, 2009), 127–54. I explain my reasons for disagreeing with this view in *The Burial of Jesus: History and Faith* (Eugene, OR: Wipf & Stock, 2024); see also Petra Dijkhuizen, "'Buried Shamefully': Historical Reconstruction of Jesus' Burial and Tomb," *Neotestamentica* 45, no. 1 (2011): 115–29.

of the Bible, but it crystallized, thanks to this thought experiment. I found that to be a positive thing rather than something negative. On one level, yes, any beliefs that one holds about what God did or did not do in the past are going to be unfalsifiable, incapable of being proven or disproven, and so should be held lightly if at all. On another level, being freed from trying desperately to prove that which simply cannot be proven is a weight off one's shoulders. Historical investigation deals in probability and normal cause and effect. It cannot pronounce on whether God acted, and at best it might declare it probable that Jesus's body was not in the tomb early on the first Sunday morning after the crucifixion. "Jesus probably rose from the dead" is not what most believers are looking for, nor is it a message many would consider compelling to proclaim. History cannot answer these crucial questions, and merely choosing to believe certain things happened in the past is not a valid alternative. One can do that in relation to *any* religious claims. As I pondered this, my faith became unmoored from where I had tried to anchor it. The result, as it turned out, was not drifting into tumultuous waters that caused my faith to capsize and sink but sailing into open waters of exploration that promised to take me to exciting new destinations.*

The next stop for the time and space machine was a few years earlier, in Galilee, to see what Jesus was like. If he turned out to be a real jerk, I felt *that* would impact my Christian faith even more directly than anything I saw regarding the resurrection. That was partly because witnessing an action is different, positive evidence,

* These issues about the relationship between faith and history were not new, although they confront individuals anew in each generation. See, for instance, David Cairns, *A Gospel Without Myth? Bultmann's Challenge to the Preacher* (London: SCM, 1960), 145; Gregory W. Dawes, *The Historical Jesus Quest: Landmarks in the Search for the Jesus of History* (Louisville: Westminster John Knox, 2000), 186.

in comparison with not seeing something happen. It was also at least partly because I was aware (on at least some level) that following Jesus is more fundamental than believing certain things about him. After all, the earliest disciples didn't have the Nicene Creed and the doctrines expounded in it. Indeed, they didn't even have knowledge of the crucifixion and resurrection. They followed Jesus, literally. If Jesus turned out to be a different sort of person than I believed him to be, that would have a profound impact on my faith.

Yet here too the result of this thought experiment was a positive one rather than something negative. It helped me to see that some aspects of my faith did not depend on unprovable claims that miracles happened. Not all of it was falsifiable. I also began to recognize that what was really on the table was revision of my beliefs, which turned out not to be the same thing as "losing my faith." I have sometimes heard people say, "If I found out Jesus didn't really rise from the dead, I'd become an atheist." I have come to find that leap puzzling. Why an atheist? Why not convert to Judaism under those circumstances? Why not pantheism or Deism? Plenty of people believe in God but not in Jesus. All beliefs within a religious system do not stand or fall together, and the evidence for one point does not necessarily support or otherwise impact another. The time-travel thought experiment helped me distinguish between my *beliefs* and my *faith*. Traveling back in time to learn about Jesus directly could cause me to revise my beliefs in lots of ways. Some of the changes might be so extensive that I would no longer consider myself a Christian. But my faith, I realized, was something deeper. A conviction about the meaningfulness of life and the richness of existence. A conviction about transcendence.

Time travel to the first century might cause me to change or shed some of my beliefs, but what would it take to make me lose my faith? The answer to that question was of a different sort entirely. If I traveled trillions of years into the future and there was nothing—no universe, no life, no God—that would shake my faith at its core. In that case, nothing would persist, nothing of the moments that are lived now would have a legacy. My specific actions do not need to be remembered for the present to be meaningful, but the idea that there is nothing in the future that was shaped by the present, no future descendants who, though no longer human beings in the modern sense, evolved from us, to say nothing of a God that at least recalls and cherishes each moment and each entity—that would indeed call into question my worldview at its most basic level. My impression of life in the present is that it is rich with meaning and has transcendent depths beyond what I can plumb. That turned out to be the foundation, the core, the heart of my faith.

I share this because, if you have been living on the pile of rubble of your previous way of thinking, you might still be hoping one day to suddenly discover you can build your worldview back precisely as it was before, or replace it with something equally certain. Alternatively, you might be convinced that there is no prospect for the future other than living with the uncertainty and instability of being spiritually homeless. You may never have cleared away the debris to see what precisely remains, and what is underneath it all. There may be individual pieces that are worth salvaging. Just because you cannot sing the songs you used to about your faith doesn't mean that music itself must go. (Indeed, one way I knew I had turned a corner in my faith journey was when I began writing songs that reflected where I had ended up, songs that did not just repeat over and over some variation on "I don't know what to believe anymore.")

More importantly, you should see what's at the heart of it all. Sometimes the foundation on which a structure was built was bad, and sometimes the ground itself was unstable. If so, then you can take a journey of exploration looking for something more stable and appropriate to build on. By this I don't mean looking for something *certain*. Such a quest is characteristic of the modern era. You'll find it at work both in science and in religious fundamentalism. It has its uses, and some validity on a smaller scale, but it doesn't work at the level of philosophy and metaphysics. Ultimately, you'll reach a level not of certainty but of *conviction*. You'll find, hopefully, that you consider other human beings inherently valuable in ways that could not be proven through a laboratory analysis of their chemical makeup. You'll find that you believe there's meaning and depth to life, or that you don't. Either way, ponder why, and whether that has changed or indeed could change. That will help you find what your foundation has been. Whether it remains the same one or you find another, your quest will lead you sooner or later to a foundation on which you can build.

Your structure will not be perfect and permanent, but one that is personally meaningful and fulfilling, one that is useful for the purpose it needs to serve in the present and near future. Houses are not indestructible. That doesn't mean they are useless in keeping out the elements and keeping belongings safe. The same is true of faiths and worldviews. Recognizing that past false certainties were illusory should not lead you either to seek others of the same sort (they'll prove equally illusory) or to shrug and say anything goes because nothing is certain. The fact that more than one thing is possible doesn't mean they are all equally likely. That is what fundamentalist systems are created to try to save people from: the hard work of weighing probabilities and drawing conclusions knowing that future evidence could force you to change your mind. That's another skill that academics cultivate, one that we ought to share more widely. It is the means by which we reach the conclusions that are the focus of our publications. The fact that we know our conclusions could be wrong, and we put them in print for all to see, shows that there's an element of *courage* required. It is possible to have convictions, to know full well that your views are not absolute certainties and yet find the courage to act on them nevertheless.

In fact, we put our ideas in print not only to share our conclusions but precisely to test them. You may have heard of peer review. On the front end of the process, this refers to the vetting of articles and books by expert readers before a publisher decides whether to publish them. The evaluators don't check that the conclusions are right, just that the methods and modes of argument are appropriate. They are making sure that the publication will contribute to the academic conversation, not that it will bring it to a close. The decision they make is not whether "this is correct" but whether "this is worth talking about." Once something is published, another kind of peer review begins, in which arguments are read and then either found persuasive or countered with other arguments. Either way, this process aims to get us closer to the truth. Each of us has limitations of knowledge, understanding, and perception. Conversation and collaboration are crucial to avoid being misled by our own limited perspectives. This quest for truth is the foundation of what academics do, and if you make something similar fundamental to your religious and spiritual journey, it allows you to relate to faith and doubt in a whole different way. Your wholehearted search for God and the truth about God can then take center stage, in place of defending beliefs you have simply accepted.

Many who read a book like this one will have experienced the collapse of a belief system that was all about assenting to propositions, about believing certain things to be true. Doubt was probably viewed as the opposite of faith, a dangerous attack on faith. When the Bible talks about faith, this is rarely the focus. One exception is in the letter of James. In 2:19 the author of that letter challenges the notion that holding to a particular doctrine such as monotheism, belief that God is one, can be all that is required to please God.

After all, the author says, demons also believe that there is only one God. Yet that doesn't mean demons are on the right track! Therefore, what you do must matter and not merely what you believe. We'll explore that point more in a later chapter. For now, let's notice the apparent tension with what Paul says, when he emphasizes that Abraham was justified by faith (see especially Rom. 3:28–4:3). There the emphasis is on trust and faithfulness, which are also part of the meaning of the word for faith that Paul used, just as they are within the realm of meaning of our English word. Abraham trusted God, and that made all the difference. Abraham trusted, I should add, without having the faintest inkling of most later Christian doctrine. If Paul were talking about justification by faith in the sense of assent that Christian doctrine is true, then Abraham could not have been justified by that standard.

Emphasis on believing certain things to be true is an effort to foster the illusion of certainty we talked about earlier. In essence, it is idolatry, making human doctrines the focus instead of a God who transcends our ability to comprehend. If being on the right track depended on getting doctrines correct, then we'd all be in equally serious trouble. If you read the Bible apart from a fundamentalist framework, you'll discover that being in a right relationship with God is never based on passing a doctrinal examination. The good news is that this means that seeking the truth about God, making that endeavor and quest central to one's life, is not only what faith can mean, but arguably what it is supposed to mean. Pursuing God wholeheartedly, pursuing ultimate truth unflinchingly, has to include precautions due to our own limited reasoning and the fact that others are equally limited. There is also the penchant for us to deceive ourselves and for others to seek to deceive us. In view of such considerations, it would be reckless *not* to doubt, to ask hard questions, to demand evidence about God if we take the subject at all seriously.

Daring to doubt, including doubting one's own ability to perceive accurately and to draw the right conclusions, becomes a crucially important positive tool in the service of faith. We're all pretty good, most of the time, at doubting what other people say, especially when we'd prefer that they be wrong. Doubting our own perception and approaching the insights of others with a balance of skepticism and openness is harder and takes a lot of practice. Here too something that academics do as a matter of course is worth sharing with those seeking a different sort of faith than the doctrinal house of cards they spent years propping up. The winds that were threatening it, once perceived as a satanic threat, turn out to have been the Spirit of God offering an invitation to a deeper and more mature faith.*

Unapologetic Faith

The English word "apologetic" has two meanings. One is closer to the Greek root of the word and means a defense of one's views. The other meaning is saying sorry for something. Both meanings are relevant here. If your experience of the former meaning is encountering (or perhaps *being*) one of the theobros on Twitter, you'll be in for a real shock to learn about the earliest Christian apologists. Individuals like Justin Martyr and Clement of Alexandria didn't work to keep the best contemporary philosophy and other learning out of their faith. On the contrary, they sought to integrate the two, because that was the way to model and promote a form of Christianity that would be plausible and persuasive in their time and place, as well as the way to have a coherent viewpoint they

* On this topic I highly recommend a book by my colleague based on a course that he helped develop which we have both taught: Brent A. R. Hege, *Faith, Doubt, and Reason* (Eugene, OR: Wipf & Stock, 2020).

themselves could find compelling and reasonable. They sought to show that Christianity was credible and worth believing not by showing that everyone else was wrong but by demonstrating that Christianity agreed with everything that was right in other systems, while also offering something that others did not. When I talk about an unapologetic faith in the sense of not feeling the need to engage in apologetics, I don't mean it in the ancient sense but in the modern. A healthy and confident faith can engage in dialogue and debate, can be simultaneously confident and open to learning and improvement. I want you to have a worldview that you can inhabit without needing to constantly be on the defensive and on the attack (things that are signs of its inherent weakness).

Because the word "apologetics" has become so tarnished, we don't tend to apply the label "apologist" to most of the serious Christian thinkers today who exemplify the best pursuit of the intellectual and spiritual life. Yet there continue to be individuals who model this ancient way of making the case for their faith by being as honest and reasonable, as caring and spiritual, as they possibly can. What I seek to offer here is a faith that doesn't need to tear down the beliefs of others in order to reinforce one's own false and dangerously smug sense of superiority. Often, when I see the behavior of self-appointed defenders of Christianity and other ideologies online, I wonder what they imagine they are accomplishing. They offer claims and arguments that aren't persuasive to anyone outside of their framework of assumptions, and they fling insults around in mean and nasty ways in the process. It makes one want to steer clear of whatever they happen to be promoting, since it fosters neither moral nor intellectual excellence. There have most likely always been such people who bring a whole religion (or culture or fan base or anything else) into disrepute. If we look for a system or community that has no such individuals, we're back to looking for something that isn't on offer among the creations of human beings. The best that we can do is to strive to do better and encourage others to do the same. As we inhabit a way of thinking and viewing the world that is persuasive to us, we should remain open to adjusting or even abandoning it if that eventually proves necessary, and do so in a way that is honest and ethical. If you look past the loudest voices, you'll find individuals of that sort in every tradition (and culture and fan base) too.

Often in the wake of deconstruction people end up with a different sort of "apologetic faith," a faith for which they constantly feel the need to apologize. I fully understand the instinct in today's climate for some to emphasize that they are "not that kind of Christian." I also wear, even if loosely, labels with qualifiers such as "liberal Christian" or "progressive Christian." The problem is that doing so risks allowing fundamentalists to define the tradition and serve as the default meaning, as though their variety is most authentically Christian and everything else is a departure from its pristine purity. That is indeed the marketing slogan for that brand of belief, and it has proven incredibly persuasive even among those outside. You only have to notice how often people in the media refer to "biblical literalists" to realize this. Whenever I hear that phrase on the news, I cringe. They aren't biblical literalists in any consistent sense.* As soon as something is too ethically challenging, or too completely implausible in light of what we know about the world, suddenly they will insist that it is a metaphor that shouldn't be taken literally.

The biggest problem with this system is that it places the focus of religious identity and fidelity on things like denial of mainstream science, whereas Jesus placed his emphasis on things like love for

* The book that played the most decisive role in shifting me away from saying "I'm still a Christian, I just . . ." to simply inhabiting a liberal Christian identity is Keith Ward, *What the Bible Really Teaches: A Challenge for Fundamentalists* (London: SPCK, 2004).

enemies, compassion, and humility. Denying evolution is much easier than the actual demands of Jesus, and so it is not surprising that some have sought to rebrand Christianity in terms of the former in place of the latter. That substitution scarcely deserves the name Christianity at all, in my opinion. It certainly isn't the most authentic form of it. Not by a long shot. Why then should we allow those with that approach to be treated as the default? They are the ones who ought to be adding qualifications. Followers of Jesus, there is significant historical agreement, ought to be characterized by radical love and self-sacrifice. All of us fail to exemplify those traits on occasion even if we aspire to them. Those who don't even try ought to be the ones to apologize and say they're "not that kind of Christian," if they are going to lay claim to the label at all.

Before Moving On (or Moving In)

Where the journey takes you next will depend very much on where you are starting from. For some this may be a whole new direction. For others, it may just be putting the finishing touches on a process that was mostly complete by the time this book ended up in your hands. The best DIY books are useful to those yet to begin a process and those trying to complete it. I hope that proves to be the case with this one.

The ends of chapters in DIY and other books that facilitate achieving your goals independently are often used to recap and encourage reflection and planning. So first, to briefly recap some key points:

- When a building or a worldview collapses, it is because of structural issues. It should not be replaced with the same type of structure before undertaking a radical investigation of what was wrong.

- All human constructions, whether physical or cultural, are imperfect and prone to collapse.
- What follows in this book is not a guide to how to finally replace your old mistaken human beliefs with the real deal—God-given beliefs that have no contradictions or tensions and so will stand forever. Those have not been provided to humankind, despite false claims to the contrary.
- Our desire for the illusion of certainty is idolatry. It reflects the human craving for an image of God that we can rely on precisely because the ambiguity and freedom of true divinity are too challenging and uncomfortable for us. Idolatry is problematic whether the image is made with human hands or with human words and ideas.
- Deconstruction (or demolition or catastrophic collapse) of a worldview is painful, but so is remaining on the rubble heap of your former viewpoint, refusing to move on. Although it can be scary to build after such experiences, it is worthwhile, and help is available (including but not limited to what you'll find in this book). You don't need to do this alone, and no one ever truly does it alone anyway.
- Worldviews are not limited to, and should not be defined by, their most obnoxiously dogmatic members.

In addition to reminding yourself about some of the points made, you should think about other things before proceeding. Perhaps most crucial is the thought experiment that I found so helpful, which I hope you will as well. Take a trip in the time and space machine.

1. What time and place will be your destination? Don't rush on to imagining going there just yet. Stop long enough to reflect on *why* you might choose to go there and then. Why is that specific

moment in history important? Should it be? What does that say about the importance of history in general in your ideology and your values? What is the significance of the fact that you don't actually have a time machine, and history cannot provide certainty about past events?

2. What might you see in the time and place you travel to? How would it impact your beliefs? What could you witness that would cause you to revise or abandon beliefs that you hold or once held?
3. Where would your second and maybe even third choice of destination be and why?
4. Finally, if you change your beliefs about those people and events, what is left that is central to your worldview? What core values would not ultimately be impacted by the revisions to these beliefs about your past?

Hopefully this thought experiment will be as helpful to you in identifying your foundation, the core of your worldview, as it was for me. Take your time thinking about it. Sit with your initial answers and impressions and give them thought. Taking the necessary amount of time is as crucial in faith formation as in the construction of a physical building. No need to rush on before you are ready. Of course, some readers of this book have been ready for a while and have just needed this bit of extra help to move into the next stage of the process. Taking too much time to do something can cause problems, just like not taking enough. Let your own experience of this process be what you need it to be, without feeling pressured to move at the same pace as anyone else.

Each of the chapters in the rest of this book explores an aspect of what faith might be. There is no need to read them in order if a later one seems to address something more pressing in your life right now. Other chapters might not address where you are at the moment at all. That's okay too. DIY books are meant to be used in a variety of ways and provide a resource to people in different circumstances. People often dip into them at different times as they undertake different projects. I recommend hanging on to books of that sort even when you periodically declutter your shelves, as they might be precisely what you need at some later point. Just as there is no one-size-fits-all faith, faith should grow and develop over the course of one's life. That isn't just true in moving beyond the kindergarten faith that is most often what comes crashing down in a distressing way. Everything in life that is alive undergoes change, and that never stops. If you have a static faith, you have a dead faith.* While the transitions from childhood to adulthood are the most dramatic, they aren't the only ones that life has in store for you. This applies to spiritual life every bit as much as physical life. If I've done what I set out to with this book, it will serve as a guidebook that you can return to more than once in your life, as well as one that you can share with people who are at a different stage of their journey than you, and have them find it meaningful too.

* Feel free to imagine a variation of the classic Monty Python dead parrot sketch here. In addition to perhaps providing a chuckle as you consider the argument that your old faith is "just resting," it also provides a nice illustration of the concept of unfalsifiability that I mentioned earlier.

1

Faith That Works

After the discovery of problems with one's earlier fundamentalist worldview brings the whole system crashing down, it can seem like there is nothing left. On an emotional level one can empathize with those former fundamentalists who simply switch into the atheist camp. If you accepted everything on authority, then when that authority is unmasked as dishonest, nothing can remain untouched. Hence the statement you'll often hear from those who have begun questioning and have pursued it relentlessly: "I don't even know if I believe in God anymore." For those for whom that is the only question that matters, let me provide some reassurance. In the next chapter I'll explain why debates about the existence of God have become a nonissue for me. I don't mean that the existence of God has ceased to matter to me. Nor do I promise to offer some knock-down proof for theism. I think the existence of God is simply beyond question, while countless questions remain and deserve to be asked about the nature and attributes of the Divine. We'll return to that in the next chapter, and see how theology can become a focus of exploration rather than dogmatism. If you can't wait, skip there and read that chapter first. I hope you'll stick with me, though, because there's something we ought to explore first: the fact that Christianity doesn't have to be about those sorts of doctrinal questions at all.

Creeds and Houses Built on Rock

It has been pointed out that the teaching of Jesus encapsulated in the Sermon on the Mount (a compilation created by the author of the Gospel of Matthew and found in chapters 5–7 of that work) is entirely about what people should do. Fast-forward a few hundred years to the fourth-century Nicene Creed, and it is entirely about what people should believe and not at all about what they ought to do.* How did we get from the focus on living a certain way to the focus on thinking a certain way? To use the technical terms (which I promise I won't repeat again), how did following Jesus get transformed from orthopraxy (acting rightly) to orthodoxy (thinking rightly)? This chapter isn't the place to narrate that part of the history of the church, which you can find elsewhere if you are interested.** It is nonetheless crucial to observe this change of emphasis because those who deconstruct their belief system often

* The most popular formulation of it is probably that by Robin R. Meyers in his book *Saving God from Religion: A Minister's Search for Faith in a Skeptical Age* (New York: Convergent, 2020), 103: "Consider this remarkable fact: In the Sermon on the Mount, there is not a single word about what to believe, only words about what to do and how to be. By the time the Nicene Creed is written, only three centuries later, there is not a single word in it about what to do and how to be—only words about what to believe." He made a similar point in *The Underground Church: Reclaiming the Subversive Way of Jesus* (San Francisco: Jossey-Bass, 2012), 20.

** Most histories of the early church tell the story of how significant debates arose early on centered on Gnosticism, Christology, and other doctrinal questions. See, for instance, J. N. D. Kelly, *Early Christian Doctrines* (New York: Harper & Row, 1960); Henry Chadwick, *The Early Church* (New York: Penguin Books, 1993); Justo L. González, *The Story of Christianity*, vol. 1 (New York: HarperCollins, 1984), 49–66; Maurice Wiles, *The Making of Christian Doctrine* (Cambridge: Cambridge University Press, 1967). That which becomes the focus of debate in one era is often passed on to the next generation as a key focus of the religion more generally.

don't know what to put in its place, and indeed sometimes feel no great urge to put anything in its place. Tracing the Jesus movement back to its early days, we discover rather quickly that another option has been there from the very beginning. It is possible for one's faith to be about doing rather than about assenting to propositions. While there is a place for rebuilding and reconfiguring one's belief system, that is just one facet of a life that includes a practical ethical focus as well.

It has become common during the past half century for conservative evangelicals to try to distinguish their brand of Christianity from other denominations and other faiths by saying, "It isn't a religion, it's a relationship." Ironic, isn't it, that the very people and churches most likely to say that also put so much emphasis on assenting to certain doctrines, and on doing or not doing certain things, as markers of their identity? (It is such internal contradictions and tensions that make it inevitable that the system cannot stand forever. Recognizing this should ultimately be liberating even if inevitably the experience is initially somewhat terrifying.) There are many reasons why the slogan that plays religion off against relationship is problematic. For one thing, any religion can say that. For another, the term "religion," while not exactly corresponding to any word in ancient Hebrew or Greek, nevertheless appears in English translations of the Bible, where it is used positively. In fact, James 1:27, as rendered in the New International Version, offers a definition of religion: "Religion that God our Father accepts as pure and faultless is this: to look after orphans and widows in their distress and to keep oneself from being polluted by the world." If you're disillusioned with your experience of religion, one option is to redefine it. Yet this is not so much an act of revision as it is an act of recovery of something that was there from the start, something precious and important yet long neglected. Imagine if this was how Christianity was defined by its adherents and recognized by those outside: Christians are those who take care of people that everyone else neglects.

The last bit of the verse sounds much more like the way fundamentalists talk. But where conservative religious people are often concerned to keep out worldly influences in the interest of preserving purity as they understand it, what worries them (and what they do about it) is very different from what we find in the letter of James. Indeed, the religion that pleases God in James is something increasing numbers of conservative Christians reject.* What fundamentalists are trying to keep out is, at least in this particular instance, what James is trying to make sure is brought in. This is made clear in the verses that follow. Because of the chapter and verse divisions that weren't originally part of the text, it is possible to read James 1:27 and stop, or to read James 2:1 without noticing what went before it. Favoritism toward the rich and embrace of discrimination are the kinds of "worldly things" that James is concerned could find their way into churches.

Fundamentalists often use purity language that is borrowed from the Bible, and they string it together with other verses lifted out of context in the same way. That thin veneer of biblical language isn't enough to justify labeling their views "biblical." The emphasis on care for widows and orphans, for those not cared for by "the world," goes back much earlier than the beginnings of Christianity. We find it in the Pentateuch's laws and in the proclamations of Israel's prophets. It is there throughout the Bible. If, as I suspect, this wasn't part of your experience of "Bible-believing Christianity," hopefully this will make

* Nowadays they are liable to label it "Communist," "Marxist," "woke," or "leftist." If one perceives even a tiny extent to which such a label might seem apt, it is because Jesus and his earliest followers pioneered practices like the sharing of belongings—see Acts 2:44–45 and 4:32–37. Marx was aware of that and selectively borrowed from what Christians had done before him when crafting his own ideology. See Alasdair MacIntyre, *Marxism and Christianity* (New York: Schocken Books, 1968).

clear that one of the serious problems with "Bible-believing Christianity" is that that label is false advertising. It claims to be something it is not. Those who most strongly identify as "Bible-believing" may read the Bible daily in their quiet time, all the while glossing over passage after passage that doesn't fit their assumptions. I know because I myself did this, and because I continue to interact and have conversations with people for whom the same seems to be true. In the interest of full disclosure, the first time I tried reading through the entire Bible, I got stuck in Chronicles, in the midst of a genealogy. As I heard from someone back when I was a student, even those who believe the entire Bible is equally inspired don't find it all equally inspiring. Academics say all denominations have a canon within the canon. Pentecostals spend more time on the passages in Acts and 1 Corinthians about speaking in tongues than others do. Lutherans and a few others spend much time in Paul's discussions of justification by faith. Even those who insist they believe the whole Bible do the "picking and choosing" they prohibit others from doing.

There are plenty of examples of Christian fundamentalists repurposing images from the Bible to mean something other than what they did in their original context. Perhaps you know the children's song that starts "The wise man built his house upon the rock." That image is drawn from the Sermon on the Mount (Matt. 7:24–27). The song's message, however, is not the message of the biblical text. In the third verse it abandons the message of Jesus and substitutes the emphasis of conservative evangelicalism. The message of the song? "Build your life on the Lord Jesus Christ." The message of Jesus? "Everyone, then, who hears these words of mine and acts on them will be like a wise man who built his house on rock" (Matt. 7:24).* Building your life on Jesus, in an

* Unless otherwise indicated, biblical quotations in this book come from the New Revised Standard Version Updated Edition.

evangelical context, doesn't mean learning to turn the other cheek, to forgive enemies, or anything else that is in view in the Sermon on the Mount. Not that those things are rejected in most evangelical churches, of course (although we've all probably seen the news about conservative evangelical pastors quoting such things and having members of their congregation object to them as "liberal talking points"). The ethical teaching of Jesus is affirmed in most cases as an important appendix to what in evangelicalism is foundational, namely, belief that Jesus died for your sins. The selfish individualism reflected in this is something else we don't notice until we step outside that framework. Getting salvation for oneself individually, getting into heaven and being sure that you will—that is the central focus—while how you treat others is important but ultimately not a deal-breaker when it comes to salvation.

Now, to be clear, I certainly don't want to replace the message of certainty about salvation with anxiety, to replace reliance on grace with reliance on effort. Once again there is another option. Central images in the New Testament focus on God as parent and on us as wayward children. Conservative evangelicalism's gospel often makes God the problem, imagined as unable to forgive unless there is payment in blood, with Jesus's atoning death sometimes referred to in evangelistic sermons as a check that pays your debt—but only so long as you say a sinner's prayer and cash it. What an appalling distortion of the gospel this is! Salvation in the New Testament is not about bookkeeping but about reconciliation, and the thing hindering reconciliation isn't God but us. The New Testament's emphasis time and again is on God bending over backward in an effort to reach and reconcile us. The emphasis is on restoring a relationship within the context of which our lives are transformed in ways that are not rigid and oppressive but life-giving and foster our flourishing. Evangelicals will use Jesus's words on the cross as supposed evidence that God could not even look at Jesus when he bore our sins, missing that (1) Jesus was reciting Psalm 22, which ends in an expression of confidence and trust in God, and that (2) sins cannot be literally, physically moved off of one person and onto another. The latter idea reflects a depiction of sin as either debt (money can be transferred) or stain (the spill gets transferred to the paper towel, as in so many commercials). Such imagery, if it is used at all, has to be understood as a metaphor for a reality that is about what we do and the ways of thinking and acting that we foster.

There certainly is an emphasis in the Bible on God despising evil. My point here is that conservative evangelicalism takes selected bits of the Bible and presents them as the whole, while neglecting large swaths of it, and the result is at best a caricature of what the Bible actually says. Evangelicalism's dominant message and metaphors are about getting us off the hook and not about reconciling us to God or transforming us into the image of Christ. To use an analogy offered by theologian Paul Fiddes, if God is like a doctor concerned with the suffering and harm caused by evil in human lives and societies, evangelicalism makes the solution the appeasement of the doctor's anger at the disease.* The point of the Christian message is not supposed to be cheap forgiveness but transformation. If we allow the medical rather than a bookkeeping analogy to predominate, we can cast aside an image of God as supposedly angry with us for being seriously unwell. God, like a physician, might be dismayed at some of our past choices that have contributed to our current illness. But the dominant lens through which we are viewed and learn to view ourselves envisages God as one who will do everything possible for our well-being—and who has guidelines for us to follow if we

* Paul S. Fiddes, *Past Event and Present Salvation: The Christian Idea of Atonement* (London: Darton, Longman & Todd; Louisville: Westminster John Knox, 1989), 70.

want to flourish. In modern American evangelicalism, the focus is almost always on individual wrongdoing and intentions, with societal evils not addressed (and in some churches explicitly denied). Yet the Bible calls not only for individuals but for the nation or church communities as a whole to change.

Before moving on, let me make sure you haven't missed the strikingly direct relevance of the imagery Jesus used (the wise man building his house on the rock) to the deconstructing/collapse and rebuilding that is explored in this book. You probably learned the song about the wise and foolish builders as a child, understood it in the manner that conservative Sunday school teachers taught you to, and as a result were convinced that you were building on the solid rock. (You probably noticed an allusion to another song there, a hymn that does the same bait and switch, using Jesus's parable and yet making the point about "standing on Jesus" rather than putting his teaching into practice.) You made a conscious effort not to be like the foolish builder who built his house on sand (which went "splat" or "crash," depending on who taught you the song). Yet here you find yourself amid a pile of rubble. It wasn't supposed to be that way. A key to rebuilding is recognizing that, while you were sold your old worldview as a package, in fact all of its items are separable. Often, after a person's experience of fundamentalism has left them disillusioned, they simply adopt a negative view of religion, of Christianity, of the Bible, and of Jesus. Doing that will not, I think, serve you well in the long term simply because few if any human constructions are entirely bad any more than any are pure goodness and truth. To rebuild something stable, it isn't a good idea to substitute the opposite of everything you had in place previously. The opposite of a poorly constructed house is not an anti-house or an upside-down one. That is why in this book we are doing something that you might have assumed to be a waste of time. We're going to go through the rubble, brick by brick, because there is a lot in there that was actually good and which it would be a shame to throw away. For those who were always told that picking and choosing is prohibited, you hopefully realize now that you have always done it. What is required is not avoiding picking and choosing, but doing it thoughtfully and deliberately, taking responsibility for your choices.

Honestly recognizing the good as well as the bad in your experience with Christianity is crucial. Atheists often miss things about the religion they left behind, such as the sense of community. You may have been genuinely loved and loved genuinely in conservative evangelicalism, in a manner that is directly attributable to the influence of Jesus's teaching and example. Why throw that away, just because that love was intermingled with other things? People are often drawn to a Christian community precisely because they find in it a kind of love unlike anything they ever experienced before. Hold on to that love while also recognizing that, if members of your community withdrew their love toward you when your views changed, they showed that they love their ideas and their rightness more than other people. That is not what we find Jesus teaching or doing in the New Testament. According to John 13:35, "By this everyone will know that you are my disciples, if you have love for one another." You can get that on a sticker or a T-shirt that also lists other options for how disciples will be known, such as doctrine, which are crossed out. (I love the fact that you can also get a sarcastically meta-T-shirt that pokes fun at the identity markers Christians substitute in place of love. The T-shirt says, "They will know we are Christians by our T-shirts.")

When someone from my Sunday school class mentioned the complete absence of anything about how one lives in the historic creeds, it inspired me to write a song that I titled "Creed." I won't quote all the lyrics here (I've shared them online in more than one place), but here is the second verse and the final choruses:

I believe in acting justly
Loving mercy, loving grace
I believe in walking humbly
With your God

I believe in treating others
As you want them to treat you
I believe that it's good to believe
But you also must do

This is my creed
To stand against injustice
To feed the poor and needy
To side with the oppressed

This is my creed
To help the broken-hearted
To comfort the afflicted
To help the tired find rest

And if you say that's not a creed
I'll say you don't know what it means to believe

This is my creed
To be there for those who sorrow
And to work for our tomorrow
As long as I may live

This is my creed
To live a life of passion
Of kindness and of compassion
Giving all I have to give

And if you say that's not a creed
I'll say you don't know what it means to believe

The point is obviously not that these are great lyrics or that it's a great song. After shaking my old assumptions down to their foundations, being able to write songs again was itself a significant milestone. When music is important to your faith and your faith changes, it often takes a while to figure out how music may or may not feature in the new direction your spiritual journey is taking you. It gets old fast if all of your song lyrics are about not knowing what to believe anymore. More importantly, if you never figure out what to believe or at least what convictions to hold, that's not a healthy sign any more than your earlier dogmatism was. Song lyrics are obviously poetic, but if there is any stickler reading this who insists that what I'm talking about in the song is definitely not a creed, I'll happily concede the point. If you want to keep the word "creed" for doctrinal statements, by all means do so. What I am aiming to convey is more fundamental: the fact that we have so few examples in early Christian writings of anything that resembles a creed. The epistles give us a few brief creedal statements, but both the epistles and the Gospels put much greater focus on what people do. The point is not to argue over what is or is not a creed, but to shift the focus onto what James (not me, the other one) defines as true religion that pleases God. If you've spent a lot of time focusing on doctrine, I expect you'll find this shift of focus refreshing.

Bodies of Doctrine and Doctrines of the Body

For some Christians, practice and actions were never the focus in a doctrinally oriented church, and their discovery of problems with those doctrines led them to doubt and deconstruct. For others, the catalyst for their loss of faith has nothing to do with doctrines, at least not initially or directly, but with hypocrisy, the disconnect between what is denounced from the pulpit and what is revealed to be perpetrated by those in leadership. It is increasingly recognized that the louder a preacher declaims particular actions as sinful, the more likely that they will soon appear in the news, having been ejected from their ministry for doing the things they were condemning, and perhaps worse. It is astonishing that the same story can repeat itself over and over again without the entire framework losing all plausibility for everyone involved. More commonly, it is a smaller handful of individuals who recognize this to be a sign that something is rotten at the core of the movement and its viewpoint. When the majority refuses to recognize what has become clear to those few, they leave, often being viewed as backsliders or apostates by those who remained behind. Conservative religionists will insist on the doctrine of inerrancy while never admitting that it is designed to defend slavery, keep women out of ministry, and in other ways maintain past norms of inequality by focusing on what ancient Christians did rather than on the principles that led them to do what they did. Such things are a feature, not a bug. Something similar happens in the ethical framework of fundamentalism, which views the world as a place doomed to destruction and judgment, focusing not on introspection and cultivation of true goodness but instead on those sins that others do that they do not, turning those into the only things that really matter and define "who is on the Lord's side." Take heart. By leaving churches that hide abuse and embrace hypocrisy, you may be shifting courageously to the Lord's side rather than leaving it (contrary to what some might have accused you of doing).

Although most Christian fundamentalists claim to affirm bodily resurrection as the form the afterlife will take, in practice they understand "the flesh" to denote the body, a separate substance that stands at odds with the soul or spirit that could be pure if not for the body's negative influence. Once again we have a viewpoint that uses biblical language in a manner that turns out to be profoundly unbiblical. For Paul (the New Testament author who most often uses these terms) flesh and spirit were not two substances, one good and the other bad. The mind needs renewal just as the body needs transformation (Rom. 12:2). The former was more urgent than the latter, something to focus on immediately (while bodily resurrection would eventually take care of the latter). Paul's terminology echoed that of Greek philosophy, but we see in many places that he ultimately affirmed the historic Jewish view of human beings and of creation. Creation is the work of a good Creator and is itself declared good. Human beings are what we might call psychosomatic unities, using a word that brings together two of the Greek words that occur in the Bible. *Psychē* is the soul or self in Greek while *sōma* is the body.

Taking a negative view of bodily existence, as though our very physicality were a bad thing, inevitably leads in unhealthy directions. Human beings have instincts woven into our DNA. Biblical authors knew nothing about our genes, and thus Christian fundamentalists make little effort to explore the implications of research in biology. These instincts of ours push us to eat and to procreate, to survive and pass on our genes to another generation. Ancient rabbis labeled these instincts the "evil impulse." Despite this label, some of them recognized that these instincts were not inherently bad. On the contrary, they are essential to human life. At the same time, they are extremely dangerous if not managed and controlled. What is bad or evil is when those impulses are not kept in check but allowed to run rampant without restraints. The reason it makes sense to talk about "self-control" (the self being controlled is the same self that is doing the controlling, which is paradoxical) is that we have biological impulses and rational capacities that are equally part of our physical existence. Paul was aware of this when he spoke about the tension human beings experience of wanting to do something yet not doing it, and of not wanting to do something and yet doing it (Rom. 7:15–20).

When natural instincts are viewed not as a healthy part of us the expression of which needs to be overseen and controlled, but as a demonic influence from outside, these aspects of the self are denied and repressed. That doesn't make the problems go away. Within a fundamentalist Christian framework, when these instincts (usually but not always sexual) are denied or repressed, they often surface in an expression that is pathological and in many instances even criminal. Strident denunciations of "the things that people nowadays do openly and without shame" are a cover for denouncers' own shame at these urges they find themselves unable to control. The reason they cannot control them is not that people are incapable of self-control. With few exceptions everyone is capable of it. It is difficult, to be sure, but ultimately we can get out of bed even if we are still tired. We can refrain from swiping a freshly baked chocolate chip cookie despite being hungry and the aroma triggering a variety of strong biological urges. Ironically, when fundamentalists denounce the secular study of biology and psychology, they reject the very resources that provide the most helpful insights into the way that our bodies, including our brains and minds, work. These insights would enable them to understand what they are experiencing and respond in a healthy and moral way. We will return in the next chapter to science as a potential positive resource for exploring faith. For now, it will suffice to say that one cannot perform an exorcism and expect it to remove desires that are rooted in our biology and thus are part and parcel of being human. That isn't how the world works. Trying to exorcise something that is a part of God's creation, instincts of a sort that we share with countless other biological organisms, treats the product of the divine will as demonic. Fundamentalism often takes its stand on matters pertaining to creation, and yet time and again its depiction of the Creator and his handiwork is blasphemous rather than pious. It is no wonder that deconstruction is so traumatic. Fundamentalism treats much that is good as evil and much that is evil as good.

When one takes a close and honest look at the laws and ethical instructions in biblical literature that pertain to sex and marriage, it quickly becomes clear that what conservatives call "biblical marriage" is nothing of the sort. Marriage in the ancient Mediterranean world was just one facet of patriarchal cultures that treated women and men not merely differently but unequally. Modern marriage in Europe, the Americas, and Australia is monogamous. Adultery is defined as either spouse having sexual relations with someone else. In ancient patriarchal marriage, including in the Bible, it was not adultery for a man to have sex with a woman other than his wife, unless she was someone else's wife. Neither polygamy (having more than one wife) nor concubinage (having sexual partners who were not wives) was prohibited. Indeed, the legitimacy of such relationships is presupposed throughout the Bible. A woman, on the other hand, was not allowed to have multiple husbands, nor any sexual partners other than the one she eventually married. The view of sex and of marriage that is presupposed in the laws of ancient Israel is focused on ensuring that the patriarchal head of household knew which children were his and which were legitimate heirs who would then inherit his property, take care of him in old age, and provide him with an honorable burial. In pointing this out, I am not making a case for reviving biblical marriage as it actually was, just to make sure my point is unambiguously clear. On the contrary, a good case can be made that the modern form of marriage is better in numerous ways. It just isn't "biblical." When one's assumption is that everything good is biblical and everything biblical is good, then the label gets applied to things that aren't in the Bible, and the Bible gets reinterpreted if it is at odds with what we know deep down to be right and true. To some, the notion that something could be better than what the Bible offers is offensive. That reaction is a clear indication of two things. First, those people have made these human writings into an idol. Second, despite claiming to defend the Bible, they clearly haven't studied it closely. When Paul and others argued for the inclusion of uncircumcised gentiles in the people of God, they weren't doing what the Bible taught. They were claiming that God was doing something new and better.*

That is, however, only one side of the picture. There clearly are biblical *principles* that had a profound influence on the development of our modern institution of marriage. Human beings everywhere have found that "it is not good" for a human being to be alone, with or without the Bible confirming it (Gen. 2:18). People in every corner of the world also either have experienced or fear the heartache of betrayal. The concept of marriage as a monogamous partnership, characterized by mutual love, trust, and effort for one another's well-being rather than one-sided domination, is something wonderful that derived at least some of its inspiration from biblical teachings. We live in an era in which the tendency is to treat relationships cheaply, as something to be tried for as long as they are enjoyable and then cast aside when that is no longer the case. Seeing through the façade of fundamentalism's denunciations of sex need not mean embracing the cheapening of it that is the main alternative in our era. There are other options. We can celebrate the pursuit of mutuality and fidelity in a manner that is as countercultural in today's secular society as it is in fundamentalist churches. It is a vision of marriage that is modern but need not for that reason be viewed as "unbiblical," since it is not antithetical to the Bible.

There are plenty of passages that affirm principles that can be applied in creative ways to our time. Affirming that it is not ideal

* The Bible itself includes examples of people being "unbiblical." The fact that such views became part of our Bibles suggests that, paradoxically, it is at least at times biblical to be unbiblical.

for people to be lonely, while also recognizing that individuals may have callings to other paths (as, for instance, celibacy in the case of the apostle Paul), we find room not merely for begrudging acceptance of same-sex marriage but also for celebration thereof as an expression of core Christian principles. It is not good for those whose biological makeup has them attracted to members of their own sex to be alone any more than it is good for anyone else. Some may be called to celibacy, whether they are attracted to members of the opposite sex or to those of the same sex. Individuals must discern a vocation of this sort for themselves. Those whose discernment leads them in a different direction from yours are not automatically wrong for that reason. Fundamentalists often quote Romans 1 on the subject of same-sex relationships, missing that the whole point of that passage is to prepare for what follows in chapter 2, where the person doing the condemning is shown to have condemned themselves. They also miss the principle Paul quotes later in Romans. It is a principle that guided Paul, and it seems equally apt as a response to those in our time who seek to impose their own narrow vision onto everyone else in their state or country. "Who are you to pass judgment on slaves of another? It is before their own lord that they stand or fall. And they will be upheld, for the Lord is able to make them stand" (Rom. 14:4).

What Then Shall We Do?

In Luke 3:10 the crowds respond to John the Baptist's proclamation with a practical question: Okay, then, now what? If he had been a Southern Baptist, he might have called for a profession of faith. Instead of telling them to come forward to make a decision, he gives them practical instructions. His instructions aren't intended as a comprehensive list, a new exhaustive set of commandments. They are illustrative. If you repent and dedicate yourself to pursuing justice, here are some of the things that that will look like in practice. John doesn't give people a pass because of the way the world is, but he also recognizes that, initially, the best one can do is work within the existing system to transform it from within. Soldiers and tax collectors are not told to quit their jobs, much less to overthrow the government and reinvent the economy so as to eliminate their current jobs. That doesn't mean that the ideal might not ultimately be for such radical changes to occur. John, however, recognizes that there is only so much individuals can do, at least until such time as the acts of many individuals create a framework for deeper change.*

In addition, not starting with oneself might encourage blaming the system rather than taking responsibility for our own part in the larger whole. It is easier to write a manifesto calling for the overthrow of the present order than to try to embody a completely different way of conducting one's own life. That's the heart and soul of the New Testament teaching about the kingdom of God. In the context of modern capitalist societies, and in particular the United States, it is profoundly countercultural to do something with wealth other than accumulate it, or to live within our means. Living with less, and repurposing our time and income so that they benefit others besides ourselves, turns out to be profoundly fulfilling and healthier as well. Those are just a couple of concrete suggestions for ways of exploring what living your faith can look like in the present day.

The words attributed to Jesus in John 18:36 have often been taken to mean that his kingdom was something spiritual, or something located elsewhere in heaven rather than here in this world. But listen to what the text actually says: "My kingdom does not

* I explore this in detail in my book *Christmaker: A Life of John the Baptist* (Grand Rapids: Eerdmans, 2024), 78–82.

belong to this world. If my kingdom belonged to this world, my followers would be fighting to keep me from being handed over to the Jews. But as it is, my kingdom is not from here." The point of these words, uttered at Jesus's arrest and confrontation with Roman power, is not about a kingdom located somewhere else, on another plane of existence, that doesn't have an impact on society. The Gospel and letters of John regularly use the language of "the world" to denote neither the planet nor its people but the present age and its way of doing things. Hence the idea of being "in the world but not of the world" and the possibility for Jesus to say that his followers "are not of the world, even as [he is] not of it" (John 17:16 NIV). The reason why Jesus's followers do not take up weapons to defend him is not that the kingdom of God is purely spiritual, but that its values are fundamentally different from those of the society around us. This is also why Matthew 26:52 depicts Jesus saying when he was arrested, "Put your sword back into its place, for all who take the sword will die by the sword." The kingdom of God is distinguished from the kingdoms of this world not by its location but by its values.

Conservative Christians are known for saying that the problems in society are a "sin problem." Yet consider how such expressions tend to be used. One will hear that most often in response to tragic gun violence. The sins of hatred, selfishness, racism, greed, and celebration of violence are obvious contributors to mass shootings. These may be found in extreme form in this or that individual, but they are also woven into the values of our culture. Yet these sins that are societal and not merely individual get little focus in conservative Christianity. The sin of self-righteousness is likely at the heart of this tendency. It is easier to condemn others for what they do than to address the things with which one's own group is complicit. It is easier to address the speck in someone else's eye than the log in one's own (Matt. 7:3–5).

John and Jesus, and their followers after them, sought to embody a different way of life individually and in community. It takes courage and dedication to seek to do likewise in our time. Courage is required to go against the flow of conservative churches and not only of the wider society. After neglecting matters of social justice, you may find it refreshing and spiritually invigorating to shift your focus there. I wouldn't be surprised if you find yourself feeling more authentically Christian as a result, too. You may also recognize a certain continuity with things that were emphasized in your conservative church context, albeit with a twist. Most conservative churches emphasize daring to be different, going against the flow, or, to use the biblical expression, being "not conformed to this age" (Rom. 12:2). They just expect you to do that in lockstep with them, as though there isn't the slightest possibility that they themselves have conformed to this world. Yet the apostle Paul was countercultural, in relation not only to the wider Greco-Roman society but also to the branch of Judaism with which he had previously been associated, and eventually to the emerging Christian community as well. That's why we find him going head to head with Peter in Antioch (Gal. 2:11). Lots of Christians in the early church considered Paul to be simply wrong, a heretic. They viewed the fact that he disagreed at times even with the Jerusalem apostles as an indication of this.

Paul was known for arguing that non-Jews could be included in the people of God without being circumcised. His opponents responded in the same way modern-day conservative Christians might. "But that's not what the Bible says!" (see Gen. 17:9–14, which is unambiguous).* For Paul, what the Bible said wasn't the only relevant consideration. To his detractors, Paul's interactions with gentiles made it clear that he was more worldly than they

* On this topic see further my *The A to Z of the New Testament: Things Experts Know That Everyone Else Should Too* (Grand Rapids: Eerdmans, 2023), 114–24.

were; his detractors were not daring to go against the flow. Paul reminds us that simply being different from mainstream society doesn't make you right, and that sometimes the conservative Christian church urgently needs to be challenged for not perceiving and being open to what God is doing. In your rebuilt faith you can continue to hone your skills at daring to be different, putting them to good use in relation to your old conservative evangelicalism, while also daring to be different from wider societal trends as well. Instead of just going with a much smaller subcurrent in relation to a larger one, or allowing your postevangelical values to simply be those of your society in your time, as a mature religious believer you need to cultivate your own ability to discern and to not give in to peer pressure when you are convinced that particular influences are unhealthy and wrong.* Sometimes those influences will be from people who don't share your faith, while at others they will be from those who do, or at least claim to.

A Hell of a Problem

Obviously shifting the focus in the way I recommend in this chapter means that you won't be shouting "the truth" at passersby in the hope they will embrace it and be saved from hell. (Or, alternatively, you won't be offering the written equivalent in the form of a tract with "four things God wants you to know"—an overly simplistic message that, despite mentioning Bible verses, corresponds to no sermon that John, Jesus, Paul, or anyone else in the New Testament ever preached.) It is ironic that this idea of salvation through doctrine has become so popular among conservative Protestants, since it turns acceptance of dogma into a work that one does to earn salva-

* Dave Tomlinson coined the term in his book *The Post-Evangelical* (London: Triangle, 1995).

tion. That's a far cry from the grace that was emphasized as central in the Protestant Reformation. As I said earlier, shifting your focus away from doctrine onto deeds doesn't mean adopting what evangelicals view as the only conceivable alternative to their message: trying to be good enough to earn your way to heaven. An exaggerated focus on rewards in an afterlife has badly distorted modern evangelicalism. The doctrine of rewards and punishments in an afterlife was introduced as a solution to the problem of evil, of undeserved suffering. We see it emerge for the first time in the book of Daniel, written at a time when the Syrian ruler Antiochus IV outlawed observance of the Jewish law. Those who continued to keep the ways of their ancestors, what they understood to be the very laws of God, were persecuted. It is one thing for bad things to happen to good people, and another for those who are most faithful to God to be singled out for the worst suffering. This took the problem of evil to a whole other level. In response to this, some thinkers suggested that not even death could prevent God from ensuring that justice was done. The dead would be raised and those who did evil would be held accountable, while those who were faithful would be vindicated.

I suspect that the author of Daniel would be dismayed to see what this idea has become in American Christianity. Today you'll encounter people who actively argue against putting any importance on improving the world or the lives of those around them, because "the world is not our home" and "our rewards are in heaven." Can you see what has happened? What was initially offered as a solution to the problem of evil is now compounding the problem! Evangelicalism's exaggerated and excessive focus on heavenly rewards also falls afoul of the conundrum that the book of Job explores so effectively. The Accuser in the heavenly court suggests that Job is righteous because he is consistently rewarded for his good behavior. Would he do what is right without reward? If he is put to the test and made to suffer, then and only then will we see what kind of person he really is (Job 1:8–11). The author of Job didn't envisage an afterlife with rewards (Job 7:7–10; 10:21–22; 14:1–15; 16:22). That work was written before the innovation reflected in the book of Daniel occurred. Introduction of rewards in an afterlife initially seemed to provide a solution to the problem. In the hands of Christians, it has instead served to exacerbate the problem in more than one way.

My own advice as a response to this distorted emphasis is (as you might have guessed) shifting the focus to trust in God. After all, no one has come up with a vision of the afterlife that doesn't eventually seem boring and tedious. (I'm actually not thinking of the vision of floating on clouds playing harps here. I love music, and learning to play a new instrument and exploring music forever seem relatively appealing compared to some other ideas I've come across!) Anything, however good, eventually ceases to be interesting. To this can be added other awkward questions about whether our eternal memory banks will have infinite capacity, and whether people will still have free will in an afterlife. (If we do, we'll mess it up sooner or later. If we don't, then what's the point of that life, and what was the point of making us initially with free will if it isn't of eternal value?) Rather than affirming knowledge about this topic, it is better to leave such matters in God's hands. Adopting the confident stance of claiming to know whether there is an afterlife, what it will be like, and who will get to participate reflects the very worst characteristics of conservative Christianity. Humbly leaving such matters in God's hands not only reflects a deeper faith and trust in God. It has the added advantage of removing potential selfish motivation for doing good.*

This raises one last thing before we move on to our next topic. If in the past your motivation both for being dedicated to your faith

* On this see further James F. McGrath, *The Burial of Jesus: History and Faith* (Eugene, OR: Wipf & Stock, 2023), 135–43.

and for sharing it with others was avoidance of hell, then you may be wondering what could possibly motivate you to pursue a rebuilt faith of any sort. You may also be wondering whether this means that you'll never have to attempt to evangelize someone ever again. If you're an introvert, the latter point may come as a relief, but either way the former may still seem like a puzzle. The answer is that of the book of Job we have already mentioned. Unless you actually want to be evil, then this is an opportunity to cultivate goodness for its own sake. My point is not that you know for certain there is no reward for doing good. Nor is it to suggest that only if we manage to avoid any recompense are we actually doing good. Sometimes we reap positive benefits from our efforts to be kind even in this life, and that is okay. The point is not expecting and so not doing it for that reason. (See Jesus's teaching about not doing good in the interest of rewards presented in Matthew 6:1–6, 16–18. That author didn't feel able to wean people off of interest in rewards altogether, and so sought to use focus on heavenly rather than earthly rewards to motivate people to work for justice and be altruistic in the here and now.)

If you previously identified things as good that you now view as evil, and vice versa, you have good reason to want to cultivate goodness and to do so in a self-critical way. This is another reason why I keep emphasizing not simply embracing a new ideology in place of your old one. Just putting your dogmatic fundamentalist proclivities into service of a different team isn't the kind of deep change we should aspire to. The teaching of Jesus and of his early followers highlights that the line between good and evil runs through each of us, rather than between our group and others. Few people actively desire to be evil. Yet in prioritizing ourselves, or our own in-group (whether defined in terms of racial, religious, national, or other identity) at the expense of others, the very act of seeking to take care of those nearest to us can become something destructive and potentially deadly. That's what evil is in most instances, at its deepest level.

People who don't go around seeking to kill people with a different shade of skin pigmentation are liable to think that they cannot be racists, and more broadly, those who don't actively wish harm on those outside their group may think that they are loving because they love those closest to them deeply and self-sacrificially. Viewing the world as a place where people who are different from you unfortunately must be sacrificed, shortchanged, or neglected in order to preserve the well-being of your own group is not what Jesus taught. Loving your enemies only when it entails no risk to you and your friends isn't loving your enemies. More fundamentally, by treating the world as a place where you have no choice but to see others harmed in order to protect those closest to you, we aren't merely resigning ourselves to the way the world is. We are *making* the world the way that it is. That's what evil is, as exposed by Jesus's teaching.

Here too I've learned something from my experience as an academic, although in this case it isn't something positive. I've seen so many colleagues gripe about the university where they teach, cynically saying that academia is all about egos and turf wars for limited funding for one's own program. Rather than working to change that, they participate in it, advocating for their department at the expense of others. These academics may be the very ones who, in their classrooms, offer critiques of capitalism and the self-interest that drives it. Christianity offers a critique of this kind of hypocrisy. While it isn't an actual quote from him, "be the change you want to see in the world" is not a bad summary of things that Mahatma Gandhi did say. Others have said it too. Martin Luther King Jr. said that "hate cannot drive out hate—only love can do that."

The point deserves to be repeated: when we resign ourselves to looking out for ourselves and those closest to us, we don't cope with the way the world inevitably is; we make the world the way that it is, we perpetuate it being like that into the present and future. I remember seeing a billboard alongside a highway reminding me that I'm not stuck in traffic: I *am* traffic. We complain about society, but we are society. One person can make a difference, if that one person influences others. Your actions can themselves be a form of "sharing your faith." As you encounter people who are suffering because they experience the worst that the world has to offer, presenting an alternative not just in words but in your lived example may provide something they are longing for.

This provides an answer to the question, should it ever arise in your mind again: "If I'm not concerned that I or others will go to hell if I don't do a particular thing, why should I bother?" Do it because it makes a difference to that person in the here and now. If you find yourself embracing the universalistic hope that sooner or later God will manage to persuade everyone to be reconciled, that doesn't make the present day irrelevant.* If you knew for certain your child will be alive and happy twenty years in the future, would that cause you not to care whether they make their lives a living hell in the present? I think I can safely assume what your answer to that question will be. I hope that you won't miss the contrast to evangelicalism's twisted focus on future rewards as though they make everything else irrelevant. Not everyone goes to that extreme, but if you've lived within that framework, you'll know the tendency that I'm talking about.

Conclusion

There are a number of reasons why this chapter seemed to be the appropriate one to place first in the book, immediately after the introduction. If you previously subscribed to a doctrine-focused faith, it is important to revisit the teaching of Jesus and realize that doc-

* For one recent case for universalism, see David Bentley Hart, *That All Shall Be Saved: Heaven, Hell, and Universal Salvation* (New Haven: Yale University Press, 2019).

trine was not where he placed his emphasis. When he emphasized *faith*, it wasn't belief that certain propositions were true, but faith in the sense of trust in God and recognition that God was at work in his own ministry. When someone who wasn't Jewish (and who thus could not be presumed to be a monotheist) came to Jesus asking that his servant be healed, Jesus did not ask the man whether he had swapped the Roman gods for the one God of Judaism (Matt. 8:5–13). Jesus's own disciples are depicted as sticking with Jesus when others had turned away, not because they understood what those who departed did not, but because they perceived that Jesus has "the words of eternal life" (John 6:68). They didn't understand what his words about eating his flesh and drinking his blood meant. They just perceived that it was worth sticking around to find out. We find the same thing to be true in Paul. He points to Abraham as an example of saving faith, and Abraham had no awareness of any doctrines about Jesus. The stories about the patriarchs feature sacred stones and sacred trees as part of their worship, things the Torah would later prohibit. It wasn't Abraham's doctrinal understanding, but his trust, and his actions based on that trust, that made him an example of the kind of faith that matters. The letter of James in the New Testament also highlights Abraham as an example, emphasizing that it would do no good to Abraham or anyone else to claim to believe—whether in the sense of assenting to propositions or in the sense of trust—and yet to not put it into practice. If your situation after deconstruction is confusion about doctrine, you are not alone, nor are you the first. The apostles were there way ahead of you. Seeking God wholeheartedly and cultivating true goodness in your inner life and your outward actions are what biblical faith is all about.

Some will feel an instinctive urge to object at this point. How can one trust in God without understanding? It is true that you cannot trust in God without some perception that there is an ultimate transcendent Reality to be the focus of that trust. In the next chapter I'll explain why I think you can be as certain about that as you can about anything. The point in this chapter (which we'll unpack further in the one that follows) is that getting doctrines right isn't ultimately possible, because no human words or concepts will ever do justice to the reality of God. That shouldn't be a disappointing conclusion. If you think you have a handle on God, what you have a handle on is by definition not God, not ultimate and infinite, and therefore not worthy of serving as the supreme focus of your life.

In the next chapter we'll see how exploring possible ways of thinking about God, possible symbols and metaphors that point helpfully in the right direction, can be an exciting and liberating part of your rebuilt faith. Anselm of Canterbury in the eleventh century summed it up in the expression "faith seeking understanding." If faith required understanding, or simply was understanding coupled with assent to the truth of what one has understood, that phrase would make no sense. What this book invites you to is not substitution of radical uncertainty in place of dogmatic claims to be certain. This book invites you to a journey of faith that can continue to grow and deepen throughout the rest of your life, one in which your beliefs may change again as you learn more. That can actually be something to look forward to rather than fear and resist, once you understand that growing and maturing is what you're supposed to be doing. The idea that you are supposed to get an initial kindergarten-level understanding of God and Jesus and then cling dogmatically to that for the rest of your life is not just bizarre and illogical, it is also unbiblical. The language of growth and deepening in maturity is there throughout the New Testament. Paul says in 1 Corinthians 13:11, "When I was a child, I spoke like a child, I thought like a child, I reasoned like a child. When I became an adult, I put an end to childish ways." That is by no means the only text that encourages Christians toward maturity. Take a look at Philippians 3:15 and Hebrews 5:11–14.

What should you do? What should your faith be like? If you focus on being a transformative influence for good in the world, that will be more than enough to keep you busy for the rest of your days. You may not even have much time to worry about matters of doctrine and things like that. Nevertheless, there is room in a rebuilt living faith not just for actions, but for beliefs, ideas, and language. They can be an exciting and important part of it. Turn to the next chapter when you're ready and we'll explore that next.

Key Points from This Chapter

- Focusing on what you do rather than what you believe is fundamentally biblical. If your religious experience thus far has been fixated on doctrine to the exclusion of everything else, and discovering problems with those doctrines caused a crisis of faith, take some time to explore the Bible's emphasis on justice, on action, on care and kindness expressed in practical ways.
- The way that human bodily existence is framed in some religious contexts is a direct contributing factor to the heinous actions by leaders that have been revealed time and time again. Changing your views on topics like sex and the body can be a step in a healthy direction.
- Phrases like "biblical marriage" obscure the huge differences between what is described and assumed in the Bible, and what so-called Bible-believing Christians today stand for.
- If you left a community because of hypocrisy or any other reason, and they shamed and denounced you for it, consider that (even if they say otherwise) you may have been stepping over to God's side rather than away from it.
- Overemphasis on afterlife has been a contributing factor to Christians ignoring biblical teaching on the importance of what we do in the here and now.

For Reflection and Discussion

If, instead of focusing on believing the right things about Jesus, you concentrated on acting like Jesus and according to his teachings, what might change? (Return to this question after doing this for a while and reflect on what did change.)

Where are there injustices in your daily experience that you can do something about? Have you noticed them before? Taken steps to address them? If not, why not? What could you do in the coming days to try to make a positive difference in the lives of those around you?

What organizations in your area are doing important work to help others? How can you get involved?

If you have joined with a community organization as suggested above, how has doing so impacted you spiritually?

2

Faith That Explores

For some readers the previous chapter came as a breath of fresh air, but I suspect others felt it was not the place they needed to go next. Although I encouraged jumping around among chapters in the introduction, I myself probably wouldn't do that, and I'm sure I'm not the only one. So if you patiently persisted through the previous chapter looking forward to this one, I hope you'll find it worth your wait. Do also know that I understand this sentiment, and experienced a bit of it myself. After all, it was your belief system that formerly constituted your faith. You understandably want a book on rebuilding your faith to help you to rebuild *that,* or at least something like it. Otherwise, shouldn't this book be called *Replacing Your Faith*? I hope that the previous chapter may, even for readers who feel that way, have provided a glimpse of the important fact that a balanced faith, a healthy worldview, needs to be multifaceted. Also, if you are not to just rebuild another flawed and flimsy structure that will collapse around you yet again, you need to rebuild your beliefs *differently.*

Since the time of René Descartes, the one thing that people in the European intellectual tradition have considered certain is that I exist. That doesn't mean the author of this book exists, but that each of us cannot logically doubt our own existence. What led Descartes to that insight was a process of radical and courageous deconstruction. He recognized that typical arguments for the existence of God or the truth of Christianity would not persuade anyone who was not already convinced of certain presuppositions, and detractors were not at all convinced of those presuppositions. He thus tried doubting everything in order to determine what was certain and build his argument beginning on that foundation. The one thing he could not doubt was his own existence, because in the very act of trying to doubt his own existence, he could not deny that there was some thing that was doubting his own existence. His own thoughts about what is certain or uncertain were themselves undeniably occurring. Hence his famous saying, "I think, therefore I am."

That's fine as far as it goes, but getting from there to certainty about the world around us is not straightforward. You can read more about Descartes, the Enlightenment, and the recent trend known as postmodernism that has called into question the possibility of being certain in the way that rationalists sought to be. The Enlightenment modernist attempt to find an absolutely certain foundation and build step by step upon it so that one ends up with a complete worldview that is certain simply doesn't work.

So is it possible to be certain about anything other than one's own existence? I promised in the previous chapter that I would come back to the topic of the existence of God. Just as faith can mean belief that certain doctrinal propositions are true, or trust in God despite having a great many uncertainties about those same doctrines, so too the word "God" is often used without definition or explanation.

The depiction of God in the Scriptures was causing some people problems already in New Testament times. A philosophical concept of God had developed that emphasized true divinity as transcendent, unchanging, and beyond comprehension. The God of the Scriptures had a body and a temper. A God who might be present in or absent from this or that location was (and still is) in tension with a God that is everywhere. Both Judaism and Christianity embraced these philosophical developments, and found various ways of making sense of the depictions in Scripture that stood at odds with notions like omnipresence or perfect benevolence. One common solution was to treat them as metaphors rather than as literal descriptions of God (which is presumably what they were originally understood to be, just as the dome in Genesis 1:7–8 was understood to be something physical that held up the waters above). The ancient Gnostics solved the problem a different way, treating the descriptions of the creator deity as literal and distinguishing that entity from the supreme good source of all. We have ample evidence of the vibrant discussions that took place about these topics among ancient theologians. Needing to be clear what one means by words such as "God" is not something new.

A progressive faith is open to developments and innovations, recognizing that they can be positive (although we always need to keep in mind that not all change is for the better). Precisely by becoming open to recognizing the different voices and viewpoints in Scripture, we can trace development across the Scriptures. Lining up texts from earliest to latest, we witness God become more transcendent. A key development was when Israelite thinkers at the time of the Babylonian exile envisaged God's throne on wheels (see Ezek. 1) and able to be with the people of Israel and Judah anywhere, and not just in the land of the God of Israel. As time has passed since the ancient Scriptures were written, we have managed to understand even more about our universe, a subject that we'll say more about later in this chapter. Its vastness is conveyed to us by spectacular images provided by space telescopes. Emphasizing God's transcendence is the only appropriate response. Yet if by that we mean, as the worship song puts it, "God of wonders beyond our galaxy," then that situates God very far away.* The universe we are aware of is

* The song "God of Wonders" was written by Marc Byrd and Steve Hindalong.

much more vast than that of the ancient biblical authors. Today if we say that God sits enthroned above the heavens, that means God is very distant indeed. The idea of God needs more than a shift of traditional language into our current scientific understanding.

If we peel back the layers of doctrine that distinguish religions and philosophies from one another, the core of what is meant by "God" tends to be the Ultimate Reality, that which has always existed and always will, which transcends, encompasses, and gives rise to everything else—including the tiny sliver of it all that includes us and of which we are aware. If that is what is meant by "God," you may see why the existence of God is no longer a matter of debate for me. That there is some Reality that simply is, that is responsible for you and me and our world being here in some way, seems as indisputable as my own existence. As sure as I am that I exist, I also find reason to be confident that I have not always existed. My existence must depend on something else that simply exists and always has. What is debatable and uncertain is not that there is some Ultimate Reality, but the *attributes* thereof. So in my view, the existence of God is beyond reasonable doubt. If the universe is what simply exists, then I'll be a pantheist. A universe of that sort would still evoke my awe to such an extent that religious language seems not merely appropriate but necessary. But from my limited human perspective, I cannot say directly or even by deduction whether the universe is eternal, whether it is an offshoot or rebirth of an earlier universe, or whether it is one of many universes all crying out for explanation. My perception does not extend so far and so deep as to be able to do more than perceive that there is a Reality that is ultimate, one that is at least as great as the universe but is quite possibly greater still.* Ultimate Reality exceeds my capacity to comprehend, as God should, indeed must, in order to be worthy of the label "God."

* Science may eventually answer some questions related to this, but it is

This line of reasoning is why there is a long tradition of theologians, mystics, and philosophers feeling no doubt about the existence of God and yet holding loosely, more or less agnostically, to any affirmations about the Divine.* Indeed, a strong theological tradition in Christianity emphasizes that any attempt to say God is this or that will by definition be wrong. "God is good"? That makes it sound like God matches some human idea of goodness. Safer to say "God is not evil," they reasoned. I'm not advocating for that particular approach, nor am I criticizing it. I am simply pointing to it, since those whose faith formation took place in the context of fundamentalism almost certainly were never told about this strong tradition of doctrinal agnosticism and caution. It is not merely Christian theology but *mainstream historic Christian theology*.** Admitting when we don't know isn't something religious fundamentalism fosters, and the fundamentalist apologists you encounter online treat it is a sign of weakness. So much worse for them and for their claim to represent Christianity. The emphasis in the New Testament is, of course, precisely that God's strength is made perfect in weakness (2 Cor. 12:9). Throughout the whole Bible, there is an emphasis on humility as something positive (see, for instance, Prov. 3:34, which is quoted in the New Testament in James 4:6).

Embracing uncertainty as a positive expression of faith is a recurring theme throughout this book. Recognizing that we are not as certain as we were taught we can and are supposed to be may be

---

no more able than any other tool of human reasoning to answer the question of why anything at all exists, why there is something rather than nothing.

* See David Hume's famous *Dialogues Concerning Natural Religion* as one example.

** If you wish to explore more, the key terms to look up are *via negativa* and "apophaticism." Don't let the foreign language terminology put you off! These simply reflect the Latin and Greek words for negation respectively.

something you've already grappled with. Most likely what is more urgently needed at this point in your journey is where to go from there. Does everything just remain a messy blur of uncertainty? The answer is not monolithic. Some things will remain that way, and ought to remain that way. Claiming certainty about doctrines that have to do with the nature of God is such ridiculous hubris that we should have realized all along that it is sinful rather than pious. Humbly surrendering to a God that exceeds our capacity to comprehend is the appropriate stance. Academic study is good at exposing when we don't know things we think we do. It is also good at making the best case possible for knowing and understanding as much as we can.

The next chapter will have more about René Descartes and his effort to place everything on a foundation that was absolutely certain. Not that his foundation—certainty about one's own existence—isn't a stable one, but one cannot get from there to certainty about everything else that matters. We need to accept that our knowledge will consist of varying degrees of certainty, that we need to weigh probabilities and sometimes act despite being uncertain. That is what faith in the sense of trust is actually supposed to mean. Accepting that we often cannot be certain, and that even when we *feel* certain, that feeling may not be justified and we might in fact be wrong, is crucial to fostering one of the practical virtues that conservative evangelicalism teaches in theory yet sometimes undermines in practice: humility. Not that there aren't many truly humble individuals within evangelicalism. But the sheer number of confident proclaimers of every wind of doctrine one encounters within and emerging from that framework illustrates my point. In practice, the push to proclaim confidently, coupled with the emphasis on right doctrine as crucial to one's own salvation, creates an environment that allows self-confidence and hubris to thrive.

Fundamentalism was a response to the Enlightenment and the rise of modern science. It claims to go against the flow by rejecting mainstream biblical scholarship and science. Yet at its heart it is very much a product of the same spirit of the age as what it rejects. Fundamentalism shares its desire for certainty. It just claims to provide a firm foundation in "the Word of God" (by which it means, not Jesus, as per John 1:1, 14, but the human writings found in the Bible, which make this stance an idolatrous one). Instead of jumping from one of these options to the other, why not consider something a bit more up to date? The philosophical movement known as postmodernism has critiqued this whole approach to knowledge, and while not all of its points are persuasive, enough are to make clear that we need to learn to live without the absolute certainty that the Enlightenment, and its rebellious child religious fundamentalism, claim to offer.* This means accepting certain things about past history as probably true but always subject to revision in light of new discoveries.

It should also mean affirming values and convictions even in the absence of certainty. The fact that you cannot "prove" that all human beings have inherent worth through some objective scientific method of inquiry doesn't mean you need to hold that conviction lightly, or that you must refrain from acting courageously on the basis of it. Valuing others is itself a form of belief. It is not a belief that altogether lacks supporting evidence, but affirming that all human beings are valuable goes beyond what can be strictly proven. On the other hand, affirming values of this sort is different

* Useful engagement with postmodernism can be found in books like Myron Penner, ed., *Christianity and the Postmodern Turn: Six Views* (Grand Rapids: Baker, 2005); Robert C. Greer, *Mapping Postmodernism: A Survey of Christian Options* (Downers Grove, IL: InterVarsity Press, 2003); David P. Gushee, *After Evangelicalism: The Path to a New Christianity* (Louisville: Westminster John Knox, 2020).

in important ways from assenting to abstract points of doctrine. For one thing, the values we hold are hopefully grounded in our own sense of who we are and our own sense of worth. Just couple that with the Golden Rule, treating others the same way you'd want to be treated, and you're basically there. That isn't proof or intellectual certainty. Morals are different from the conclusions of scientific study. Making room for a practically focused faith doesn't mean becoming unconcerned about matters of truth and investigation. It means making room for other ways of knowing besides intellectual arguments.

If you've developed a certain skepticism regarding the idea of different ways of knowing, I can empathize. Some have used that language to import ideas into their worldviews for which there is little or no evidence—or worse still, against which there is a mountain of evidence. Yet hopefully your life experience has been rich and diverse enough to know the power of a novel to bestow insight and to move you to tears even more powerfully than some true stories (to say nothing of mathematical formulas or scientific equations). Hopefully you have felt lifted beyond mundane existence by music. In the next chapter we'll turn our attention to the experiential aspect of faith. For the present, I am bringing things like music and the way it affects us emotionally into the picture because it illustrates that reality has different levels. What provides adequate analysis at one level may be wholly inadequate on another. A description of your favorite music in the form of a list or a graph of the mathematical frequencies of vibration is a good example of this. An analysis of the chemical composition of the musical instruments is another. Neither of those would be incorrect in any way (assuming no mistakes have been made in the analysis, of course). Yet neither captures the experience of listening to music, of having it do something in your inner self to which words cannot do justice. In the same way, our very selves are describable in terms of subatomic particles, then atoms, then molecules, then cells, and so on up through a range of levels, each of which is perfectly valid and each of which fails to convey what is happening on a still higher level, including your existence and mine as whole persons.

This idea of emergent properties illustrates one way to envisage God in conjunction with a universe that can also be described in scientific terms. If God is not a separate reality from the universe, but is all that is (including but not limited to that which makes up our material universe) on its most transcendent level, then there is no need to "make room for God" in the scientific universe any more than there is a need to make room for you as a person in your body. You are more than the sum of your parts, but that doesn't mean you are separate from the individual cells and molecules and so on. Looking for God in the gaps between phenomena and explanations, on this view, turns out to be misguided.

Imagine two cells in your body having a conversation about the meaning of their existence. One says that it is all meaningless: cells are born and cells die, and that is it. The other wonders if perhaps they are all part of one big cell. The second cell cannot imagine what it is like to be a multicelled organism. That level of existence is literally unimaginable from that perspective. Yet its perception of transcendence and of higher levels of organization is not completely wrong either, and it intuits and finds language to express something that the first cell misses entirely. In much the same way, God is unimaginable to us as human beings. Yet it would be misguided to argue for or against the existence of God as though God were just another object within the universe that might or might not exist. That would be like the cells debating whether there is a supreme cell that might or might not exist somewhere within the body, rather than on a whole other level. Just as a cell has no higher level of transcendence to relate to than cells and so uses that imagery, we tend to think of God in personal terms. Yet God is as much beyond anything we can imagine than we are to our cells if our cells could imagine.*

What I have written thus far hopefully sounds far more speculative and tentative than the fundamentalist theology you were exposed to. That is a key difference between what you had and what I want to help you build in its place. The difference between this sort of theology and fundamentalist theology is not that one is certain and the other is sheer imagination. It is that one is honest about its character as a human activity, and its use of symbols and other nonliteral speech as the only means of talking about the Divine, while the other engages in false advertising. Fundamentalist theology is presented confidently as truth by those who market it, just as a used-car salesman assures you that you can rely on the vehicle they are seeking to persuade you to purchase. As I emphasized in the introduction, whether you are acquiring a car or a religion, you need to be skeptical of the sales pitches and look under the hood. Some fundamentalist theology, on close inspection, turns out to be profoundly problematic. In other cases, the issue may not be the imagery itself but only the insistence that it was a literal description. Theology, when you are honest about what it is, can become something exciting. We do not have a collection of revealed dogmas delivered once for all to remain unchanging forever after. We have human attempts to point to the God who is beyond what any human words can express, much less capture. As our understanding of the universe and of ourselves expands and deepens, theology can do so along with it. Rather than having to defend antiquated dogma against new knowledge, you can embrace learning, knowing that your theology can—and is sup-

* Here the language used by Arthur Peacocke, Hans Küng, and others may be helpful. They emphasize that God is "at least personal" but "more than personal." See Arthur Peacocke, *Evolution: The Disguised Friend of Faith?* (West Conshohocken, PA: Templeton, 2004), 104.

posed to—grow along with it.* Rather than merely repeat language of the past, you can draw on those historic resources while finding new metaphors and analogies as well.

The reason you were given a different impression in the past is that much conservative religion is idolatrous. It makes an image of God in words rather than stone or gold, but the aims and effect are the same. All idolatry is an effort to make humans feel safe by locking in God's presence in our midst and making people feel certain about who God is and what God does. The true God cannot be constrained and contained in that way, and hopefully you view the very attempt as ludicrous now that you can view it with hindsight. The exciting news is that, whereas fundamentalists may have told you that leaving their understanding of God behind is abandoning God, you've actually said good-bye to an idol and have entered that frightening wilderness where time and time again those who have sought after God have had an awe-inspiring life-changing encounter. I'll say more about the experiential aspect in the next chapter. For now we'll keep the focus on the fact that new experiences of God call out for new language. Like trying to speak of love, religious language is poetic and full of symbolism. For fundamentalists, the fact that language of that sort is evocative rather than restrictive is a shortcoming. For those who seek a real encounter with the real God, the multifaceted and possibility-opening character is a sign that the language is working, doing what it is meant to: expressing that which we find to be inexpressible, and pointing us in the right direction to seek and encounter God ourselves, even though we too are destined to find ourselves unable to do justice in human words to that experience.

* There is a great passage on being open to new ideas in Philip Gulley, *Unlearning God: How Unbelieving Helped Me Believe* (New York: Convergent, 2018), 176–77.

Science as a Tool for Faith Reconstruction

If you were steeped in an antiscience stance as part of your faith, then evolutionary biology, astronomy, geology, and other areas of science may have been either enemies of your faith or things that you believed support it so long as they are interpreted "correctly" (i.e., not in the way mainstream scientists in their global atheistic conspiracy understand them). By now I am guessing it is old news that your young-earth creationist teachers misled and misinformed you about these fields of scientific inquiry. In the context of your past faith, you may have avoided or at least neglected reading works about science by actual scientists. Being warned that science and atheism are in cahoots often has that effect. As a result, you not only held mistaken notions about the actual conclusions of science. You were never encouraged to read scientists like Francis Collins, who headed up the Human Genome Project before stepping into the role of director of the National Institute of Health for a while, and who is an evangelical Christian.* Fundamentalism is threatened by progress in knowledge; it tries to defend the ancient assumptions of biblical authors as though they were divinely revealed truths about the natural world. You may be surprised to learn that there are loads of Christians involved in scientific research, some of whom have written about how their awe-inspiring work in science helps rather than hinders their dedication to an awe-inspiring God.

* Francis Collins has written several books about his effort to integrate science and faith in his own life, the most famous of which is probably *The Language of God: A Scientist Presents Evidence for Belief* (New York: Free Press, 2008). Collins's evangelical approach to this is still rather traditional in comparison with what others have dared to try. Kenneth Miller, John Polkinghorne, and in an earlier generation Pierre Teilhard de Chardin are among the many who have worked in science and sought to offer theological reflections on their work and its significance.

Collins is only one of them. Pierre Teilhard de Chardin, Kenneth Miller, Arthur Peacock, Ian Barbour, John Polkinghorne, David Wilkinson, and many others likewise deserve to be mentioned.

Carl Sagan wrote in his book *Pale Blue Dot,* "In some respects, science has far surpassed religion in delivering awe. How is it that hardly any major religion has looked at science and concluded, 'This is better than we thought! The Universe is much bigger than our prophets said, grander, more subtle, more elegant. God must be even greater than we dreamed'? Instead they say, 'No, no, no! My god is a little god, and I want him to stay that way.'"* For a young-earth creationist the images from the Hubble and Webb telescopes are a problem to try to explain away in relation to their assumptions about the Bible. For those who have been liberated from or have never been burdened with that oppressive framework, such images become an inspiration.** Sagan's "hardly any" scarcely did justice

* Carl Sagan, *Pale Blue Dot: A Vision of the Human Future in Space* (New York: Ballantine Books, 1994), 50.

** If you had the good fortune to never become acquainted with this viewpoint, young-earth creationists insist that God created the heavens and the earth (as per Gen. 1) roughly six thousand years ago. The nearest galaxy to Earth, visible with the naked eye, is the Andromeda Galaxy, some 2.5 million light-years away. A light-year is a measure of distance equivalent to 5.88 trillion miles, because it takes light one year to travel that far. This means that we are now seeing the Andromeda Galaxy as it was two and a half million years ago. Since that is more than six thousand years, young-earth creationists spend their time bringing Christianity into disrepute by making unfounded claims about God creating such objects with the light already en route, or about the speed of light having been different in the past, while those who don't adopt their problematic and selectively literal approach to Genesis 1 can simply allow the heavens to declare the glory of God (Ps. 19:1), because we accept the Bible's overall teaching that the creation testifies truthfully about the Creator (Rom. 1:20). Psalm 19:1 mentions the dome of the sky showing God's handiwork. Rather than treating the discovery that the sky is not a solid dome as a threat, most Christians simply apply the principle to our better understanding of the natural world in a much more sensible and appropriate way.

to the vibrant traditions of faith and theology that did indeed look at science and conclude that God is greater than we previously imagined. As the cosmos has grown, our concept of God has grown with it. Or at least, it should. If we just add scientific information to our worldview without adapting our theology, the result is still a changed view of God, but the result may be less satisfactory.

The dome of the sky mentioned in Genesis 1 had already been replaced with multiple heavenly spheres by the first century. When Paul refers to the "third heaven," he is showing that he simply took this progress in thinking about cosmology for granted. Neither view of the world and the heavens is ours. The view that took the sun, moon, and visible planets to correlate with heavenly spheres still didn't locate the highest heaven all that far away from our terrestrial abode. Now with the vastness of space revealed by high-powered telescopes, if God is outside it all, then God is much farther away than merely "beyond our galaxy" and Jesus's ascension to heaven, if taken literally, still hasn't gotten him there even if he has been moving at warp speed.* A grander and greater view of God as the one that encompasses it all is called for, one that in fact has strong continuity with ancient theologians and mystics. Fundamentalists complain about scientists and science as though they are an isolated thorn in their flesh. In actual fact, all areas of human learning including philosophy and theology are united in calling the slightly

* This statement paraphrases something said by Keith Ward in *The Big Questions in Science and Religion* (West Conshohocken, PA: Templeton Foundation Press, 2008), 107: "We now know that, if he began ascending two thousand years ago, he would not yet have left the Milky Way (unless he attained warp speed)." I also find helpful in this context a statement by my doctoral supervisor, James D. G. Dunn, in "Myth," in *Dictionary of Jesus and the Gospels* (Downers Grove, IL: IVP, 1992), 568: "To demythologize the ascension is not to deny that Jesus 'went to heaven'; it is simply to find a way of expressing this in language which takes it out of the realm of current or future space research."

more benevolent version of Zeus offered by fundamentalists what it is: not merely an idol that makes God in humanity's image, but an antiquated one that is long past its expiration date.

Trying to selectively deny some science in the interest of maintaining the scientific truthfulness of the Bible simply won't work. You would have to deny not only the major conclusions in the field of biology but also the findings in geology, astronomy, and many others. The dome in Genesis 1:6–8 isn't there, and that is old news at this point. Discovering that hasn't troubled most religious people since we have known that to be the case. Religious and atheist fundamentalists have both had a vested interest in depicting religion and science as at war in a manner that grossly misrepresents history.* The way they have made a fuss about various scientific fields and conclusions has distracted from the many positive efforts to explore how Christian (and other forms of) faith can be reexpressed and reinterpreted in relation to these scientific developments. It's a process that goes all the way back to Paul, if not earlier. In referring to the third heaven in 2 Corinthians 12:2, he shows he has embraced what came to be labeled the Ptolemaic view of the cosmos. Rather than insisting that there can only be one dome over a flat earth as found in the Jewish scriptures, he embraced the Greek view that the earth was a sphere with seven celestial spheres around it corresponding to the sun, moon, and five visible planets.

We cannot stop there. We must continue the process of updating our view of the cosmos and allowing our view of God to expand and adapt right along with it. For those who try to inject God as an explanation for those things we do not yet understand,

* On this, see Derrick Peterson, *Flat Earths and Fake Footnotes: The Strange Tale of How the Conflict of Science and Christianity Was Written into History* (Eugene, OR: Cascade, 2021).

this ends up being a constant retreat. For those who don't take that approach, a religious framework is called for by the mysterious fact that anything exists at all, and thus something simply exists and always has. Calling that which has always existed "God" is the historic viewpoint. As I said earlier, if it were to turn out that the universe or the multiverse is that which simply exists, then one ends up being a pantheist. For that reason I sometimes tell people that I am at the bare minimum a pantheist. Even if what simply exists is the universe itself, that's still an awe-inspiring wonder that I find to merit expression in religious language. (My long-standing response to Richard Dawkins's characterization of pantheism as "sexed-up atheism" is to ask why, if one has a choice between atheism and sexed-up atheism, one would ever prefer the former over the latter.)* Yet I have no reason to think that the universe is what simply exists, nor all that exists. The mystery seems larger and deeper. I need a different category, a larger framework. I find what I am looking for in panentheism, which means that God is the all-encompassing reality within which subsist any universes there may be, while God is more than that. Whether God is more in the sense of something additional beyond and between, or in the sense of a higher level and order of meaning and coherence of the whole, is a question that I can't possibly hope to answer from my limited human perspective, and neither can you nor anyone else. So I respond with humility, awe, wonder, and reverence, and fum-

* The statement comes from Dawkins's *The God Delusion* (Boston: Houghton Mifflin, 2006), 40. There has been a lot of critical response to Dawkins by both religious people and atheists or agnostics who balk at his oversimplifications and caricatures in how he treats religious topics. See, for instance, Ronald Dworkin, *Religion Without God* (Cambridge, MA: Harvard University Press, 2013). On the other hand, Ross Douthat oddly takes Dawkins's phrase as having been intended as a compliment (see his book *Bad Religion: How We Became a Nation of Heretics* [New York: Free Press, 2012], 223).

ble about for imagery that can point to that transcendent reality that I can perceive but cannot grasp.

Hopefully, after being told things with great confidence by preachers whom you now recognize to have misrepresented the Bible, science, and much else, you'll be inclined to turn to expert sources when informing yourself about any subject. That's why I draw on and seek to integrate what scientists conclude into my worldview, rather than proffering my own opinions about science as though others should rely on them. It isn't only those who write about theology who are prone to get things wrong if they don't stick to their area of expertise. For instance, Richard Dawkins is an excellent source of information about his field, biology. If you read what he writes about religion and philosophy, you'll likely find him disappointing. I'm not saying that because I'm a Christian—atheist philosophers and scholars of religion for the most part view him the same way. Just as he would want someone like me to rely on what actual biologists conclude if I write something that intersects with biology, the reverse is equally true. Hopefully this makes clear that each of us should be resigned to knowing a lot about one or some areas and not having equal insight into all others. No one human being can know everything. That is a biblical and widely realized, practical truth. No field of study is completely isolated from all the others, and we need people who do interdisciplinary work and who seek to synthesize swaths of knowledge that span different fields. However, the further we try to extend our reach, the more crucial it is to be humble about our own abilities and to rely on the expertise of others. Some people do manage to learn so much on their own that they develop genuine expertise. Such autodidacts have made genuine contributions in lots of areas. The problem is that some people have Googled and read a bit and think they have a grasp of a matter that is more complex than they realize. In this book I'm not trying to offer definitive answers about the details of how science and theology should integrate into a worldview. Even as I write this, data from the Webb telescope has raised the possibility that long-standing assumptions in physics and cosmology may need to be rethought. Science changes, almost always for the better as our understanding plumbs deeper and sees further than others did before us, by standing on their shoulders. This book is an encouragement to explore, perhaps to even contribute in meaningful ways to the process.

When we see the renderings that a computer can offer of the shape of the visible universe, the way galaxies extend in all directions, we see shapes emerge reminiscent of neurons. It would be foolhardy to jump from that impression to confident assertions about the universe being a living thing, or anything else of that sort. Yet it also seems wrong to dismiss such evidence as though it didn't point to us being part of and within something much greater than ourselves that we can never fully understand. We will never see the universe from outside, nor know what it might be like to be a universe with all its constituent parts. Is it appropriate to suggest that those who have looked for God either in the spaces in between matter or outside of our physical universe are perhaps looking in the wrong place? If you look for the author of this book, you can go through my body cell by cell trying to find "me." (In case it isn't obvious, let me also add an explicit disclaimer that I sincerely hope you will not in fact do this.) You will not find James McGrath in any one component part of me nor in the spaces in between. I am the whole, functioning together. I am at the same time inseparable from all of the cells that are part of me. To echo Acts 17:28 (which claims to quote Paul, who in turn was quoting Epimenides), in me my cells live and move and exist. Separate them from me and they die (and remove them all and I too am no more, hence my concern lest anyone disassemble me in an effort to locate the essential me!). The image of the cosmos (or the multiverse or whatever) as akin to God's body has been around a long time, and continues to be explored by theologians within the Christian tradition as well as others.* Taking it as anything other than a symbol, a grasping for an analogy that can serve to point in the direction of a Reality beyond our ability to grasp, is asking for trouble. But that is true of all human language, and is certainly no less true than in the case of imagery depicting God as though God were one being among many in the universe. If we are to use language at all and not just remain silent about transcendent matters, then we have no choice but to use analogies and symbols, and to use them humbly with explicit recognition that they are not offering literal descriptions.

Shall We Pray?

If you have recognized the problems with imagining God as singling out individual human beings for miraculous help finding a parking spot at the mall while others suffer in famine and plague, praying at all may have gone out the window. It took me a while to figure out whether prayer would continue to be a meaningful part of my devotional life, and if so how. This too is not some new progressive idea. Ancient Christian theologians emphasized that God will always do what is best and thus prayer, if it influenced God, could only make things worse! There is thus a long tradition of recognizing that prayer is about changing us rather than changing God. In my own experience, prayer has been crucial to perceiving

* See, for instance, Sallie McFague, *The Body of God: An Ecological Theology* (Minneapolis: Fortress, 1993), 179; Maurice F. Wiles, *God's Action in the World: The Bampton Lectures for 1986* (London: SCM, 1986), 35. For a perspective critical of this analogy, see Christopher Southgate's chapter on divine action in the volume he edited, *God, Humanity, and the Cosmos: A Textbook in Science and Religion*, 3rd ed. (London: Bloomsbury, 2011), especially 234–84.

my own flaws and shortcomings. Prayer keeps me from thinking that I am the focus in terms of either how things are going in life or where solutions will come from. Reaching out beyond ourselves is an important exercise, as is dialoguing with the Ultimate even if we admit it actually bears very little resemblance to a conversation when we do so. Plus, I don't know for certain that prayer does not in fact accomplish something beyond this therapeutic level. If all things hang together in a manner that resembles organic life even by way of remote analogy, then crying out for help might, like the distress of cells in our body, trigger the greater whole into action, a response from the universe's immune system, if you will. If one continues petitionary prayer, I think the most crucial thing is to develop a practice of being thankful, instead of thanking a personal anthropomorphized deity for personally singling you out for favor. If you find that for you no form of petitionary prayer can entirely avoid the abhorrent idea that this one individual survived the plane or car crash because they prayed a little harder, had slightly greater faith than those around them, or God simply likes them better, then it may be better to not do it at all until further notice.

The book of Job is once again the place to turn to disabuse ourselves of such notions. There we learn that neither Job nor his friends were in a position to interpret their good fortune or their misfortune correctly. Nevertheless, when we read about Job crying out in lamentation, articulating complaints about God's injustice, we see that there is room for forms of prayer or at least prayer-like expression of a kind that are largely omitted from conservative Christian spirituality. It is important to find a spiritual outlet for these things. Not giving expression to them is unhealthy for our emotional, moral, and spiritual lives. If in this instance giving voice to our feelings is important and appropriate, there is no reason this should not be the case for our hopes as well as our fears, our gratitude as well as our dismay.

Two Views of God and the Cosmos

There are two seemingly incompatible images for God's relationship to the world that I find meaningful and helpful. It is not a good idea to resort to labeling contradictions in our thinking as paradoxes too quickly. Sometimes doing that is simply an attempt to shield our ideas and our shoddy reasoning from close scrutiny. Sometimes we really do need to rethink and let go of one of the two things we have been maintaining in tension. Sometimes we have unexamined presuppositions that create tensions in what we build upon them, and those presuppositions are deeply problematic. Apparent contradictions in our thinking deserve a close inspection. On the other hand, the universe itself includes paradox at the deepest level we have managed to perceive, and it seems inevitable, and entirely appropriate, that our symbolic language about God will not all mesh together. Living with paradox may be as important to a healthy intellectual and spiritual life as living with uncertainty. If we have only one tidy image of God, we have an idol that fits neatly in human boxes. If self-contradiction is a warning sign, so too is having a way of thinking and speaking about God that appears to tie up all loose ends. God is by definition too great for that to be possible for human beings.

I emphasize these points because, as I share another view of God and creation that I love, I wish to be up front about the fact that I am aware of the tension between this one and the one I had already been sharing. Reading Protestant theologian Jürgen Moltmann made me aware of the view of creation in Jewish kabbalah mysticism.* Often referred to using the term "tzimtzum," it notes that the traditional view of God as creating out of nothing poses a conundrum. If God is infinite, then how can there be any "noth-

* Jürgen Moltmann, *God in Creation* (London: SCM, 1985), 86–87.

ing" out of or into which God then creates? God is omnipresent. There is no room for "nothing"! Tzimtzum thus envisages God retracting from an area of space, withdrawing for there to be room into which creation can come into existence over against God. One might think of this as akin to a divine womb within which the cosmos is conceived and gestates. You can probably see why I like this imagery. It is a picture of God *making room for us*. If your past view of God was as a parent who expects you to remain infantile forever, this image will likely be a helpful one for you. The Protestant pastor Dietrich Bonhoeffer wrote things that fit together nicely with this image of creation. Just as it is not the aim in conceiving a child that the child remain in the womb forever, neither is it the aim that the child remain perpetually in a state of immature dependence. We want our children to grow and flourish as mature individuals. According to Bonhoeffer, that is what God wants too, that we learn to live without turning to God to resolve everything for us.*

One of these images has God equally near to everything in the cosmos, or rather, everything in the cosmos equally cohering within the reality of God. The other has God withdrawing to make room for us to exist independently. I appreciate both, and I suspect there is truth in both, just as I am sure that neither is a literal description of God and of how God relates to the material universe. The point is not that one is right and the other wrong, or that both are partly right and wrong. Both do the work that theological language does, the only work it can do, and the work only it can do. It points poetically in pictures painted with human words and images toward a Reality to which we sense we are connected, and yet from

* See his correspondence with Eberhard Bethge from June 8 and 16, 1944, published in his *Letters and Papers from Prison* (London: SCM, 1967). For many it was John A. T. Robinson, *Honest to God* (London: SCM, 1963), 39–50, which drew our attention to this important contribution by Bonhoeffer as well as related points made by Paul Tillich and others.

which we feel distant. Whether one, both, or neither of these images proves meaningful and helpful to you in your own process of constructing a worldview is less important than that I direct you to the path and process of seeking symbols that can do similar work for you as these do for me.

If you were previously exposed to theology that was supposed to offer literal truths about the divine nature, which you were then told to accept and affirm without question, I invite you to explore the power of poetry to help you explore that which you and I have no chance of grasping or articulating literally.* I also invite you to make room for ways of thinking that you hold in tension when pondering anything that is deep and wondrous in life. We human beings are ourselves multilayered, multifaceted, and at times paradoxical. It isn't surprising that the same should be true of the Ultimate Reality in which we live and move and exist. Thinking about the tensions in being human is especially helpful in relation to images of the divine drawn from our own experience and analogy with ourselves. We too are inseparable from our bodies and yet so much more than the sum of our constituent cells, just as our cells are so much more than the molecules that make them up. So it goes up and down the levels of existence as far as we have managed to peer. Our minds are inseparable from our bodies, and yet we still find it natural to speak of "mind and body" or "body and soul" as though they are distinct. A lot of fundamentalism seeks to diagram,

* I hesitate to recommend poets since different ones resonate with different people. Whether it is verses of George Herbert such as "Love" and "The Altar," Walt Whitman's spiritual explorations such as "Spirit Whose Work Is Done," or the Sufi compositions of Rabia or Rumi, Bhakti poetry by Mirabai and Akka Mahadevi, and others outside the Christian tradition, spirituality and poetry coincide in ways that never dictate but invite, even if in ways and directions the composers of the verses in question may not have intended or anticipated. Works from other traditions, precisely because evocative rather than dogmatic, provide a useful and engaging resource.

list, and define things from salvific doctrines to the events of the "end times." If you need a "doctrine fast" after that, it might do you good. But ultimately just as the solution to unhealthy eating is not refraining from eating altogether but healthy eating, this book invites you to begin to work healthy theology into your "diet."

Biblical Studies and the Life of Faith

I emphasized in the introduction to the book that biblical scholars have been "deconstructing" for as long as the modern academic study of the Bible has been around. Indeed, one might even say that deconstruction came first. The Enlightenment awareness that things we have long believed may be wrong and deserve scrutiny served as an impetus to ask hard questions about religious authority and the Bible. Yet the Enlightenment in turn owes a lot to the Protestant Reformation's challenge to traditional religious authority. It was a natural direction for things to go. Once one treats the pope and the church as capable of being wrong, deserving of scrutiny, and needing at times to be challenged, it cannot be long until someone points out that the same is true of the Bible. Fundamentalism is a last-ditch attempt to save a "paper pope" from being called into question, and yet it offers no persuasive basis for doing so other than our idolatrous desire for certainty, which is not an anchor that can hold against the storms of critical thinking for long. Most of this process is in the past for mainstream and mainline Christians, who have long since recognized and worked on the need to build a worldview that embraces new science and a radically altered view of authority, without finding this to imply the need to cease to be Christian. One way of viewing deconstruction is the fast-paced collapse of a few flimsy bulwarks against a current of intellectual inquiry that peaked a century earlier and has since subsided. The good news is that when one leaves the fundamentalist silo, one doesn't actually find a barren post-Christian wasteland but a vibrant ecosystem of diverse communities and views from which you can learn how to live as a follower of Jesus in the post-Enlightenment and postmodern era.

Yet if you recap that whole history in a matter of years, compressing a turbulent period in history into an intense individual experience, it is not surprising for it to be traumatic. Lots of people are still going through this now as the Internet and other influences have broken through fundamentalist barricades that attempted to keep out other perspectives that challenge traditional views and authority. Those who undertake academic study of the Bible have been doing it even before the Internet. Often without realizing it, people whose faith led them to pursue a degree that includes biblical studies were letting in that which their fundamentalist environment had been seeking to keep out. Some such individuals went to educational institutions where conservative bulwarks were in place. But there are deliberately made holes in those bulwarks, and they can let in light from outside. Conservative biblical scholarship has to engage with liberal and moderate views in order to do some semblance of research and offer an education. The "conclusions" are predetermined in advance, of course, in a way that calls into question whether those things deserve to be called "education" and "scholarship." That's a matter we can set aside here. The point is that the ideas that conservative professors and the authorized readings they assign interact with and quote from more mainstream scholarship. It may become clear to you then and there that what was being argued against was richer, deeper, and more persuasive than what was being argued for. That experience has led student after student to pursue further study, with their understanding of the Bible changing dramatically as a result.

Not all or even most biblical scholars have followed the precise path that I have and that this book invites you to. Some have doubled down on the beliefs they are convinced they are supposed to hold, even when the Bible itself seemed to be pointing in a different direction. Some had their views change, but could not acknowledge it because it would have cost them their jobs. Often that leads to a loss of faith due to the need to live a life of hypocrisy in the interest of providing for their family, something that they may never admit to anyone else. I am deeply saddened whenever I think about that, because that could easily have been my own experience. I was in such a setting long enough to know how toxic it would have been not only to my faith but also to my ethics, since you cannot foster the latter while needing to be dishonest on a daily basis. Still others compartmentalize, publishing things they would never talk about with people in their church. For them, the fact that so many Christians are happy to ignore biblical scholarship is a cause for relief rather than frustration. As for me, I continue to be humbled and honored that my own church is an exception in this regard, with many of my fellow members being genuinely interested in reading what I write.

I am by no means the only biblical scholar to try to integrate scholarship with faith, but it was important to mention that this is not the only path that individual scholars follow. Even as I am persuaded (as I emphasized earlier in this chapter) that we need to make room for different ways of knowing and different perspectives on the same reality, I am also persuaded that we should not try to "protect" our faith from academic study any more than we should try to "protect" the doctrine of inerrancy from the Bible.* For Christians in general and Protestants in particular, the Bible

* Ian Barbour's four ways of viewing the relationship between religion and science (conflict, independence, dialogue, and integration) are more widely applicable to the relationship between religion and academic study more generally. The four models are found in a number of his publications, including *When Science Meets Religion: Enemies, Strangers, or Partners?* (New

is supposed to be a major source of authority. If the only way for it to function in that way is to avoid careful study of it, study that pays close attention to its details and asks awkward but necessary questions about it, something is deeply amiss. One of the biggest lies of fundamentalism is that it claims the Bible as its authority while refusing to be honest about what it says, or to even listen to those who've dedicated their lives to studying it.

The idolatrous fundamentalist quest for certainty is undermined when you discover that the New Testament authors were not inerrant, and neither are their writings. Ultimately, for those who move out of fundamentalism, this reality about the Scriptures makes these texts more powerful, not less. That is when we are freed to discover what these writings are, which in turn leads to understanding them better. Many of the Bible's so-called puzzles have nothing to do with the meaning of a text being unclear. They are puzzles only for fundamentalists because a given verse seems to be saying something very different from what other verses say. The solution to the problem was right under our noses the whole time. Stop telling biblical authors what they are and are not allowed to say. Stop telling them they must all agree with one another. When we realize that this is what we have been doing, we realize that the fundamentalist may claim that the Bible is their ultimate authority, but in practice it isn't. In fundamentalism the doctrine of inerrancy, and ultimately the individual interpreter who is convinced they are hearing what God says in Scripture, are the ultimate authority, to which the Bible must bend whenever its contents resist being forced into the framework of their assumptions.

The Scriptures were clearly shaped by their times in ways that prevent them from simply providing authoritative answers to to-

---

York: HarperCollins, 2013). There he explores what each possible relationship looks like in practice in different scientific fields.

day's problems. That isn't something that is wrong with these ancient texts. What is wrong is when people assume or pretend that this is not the case! When we look at them as human texts of their time, that is when they really become interesting. It should be completely unsurprising that texts from two thousand years ago don't know modern science. That isn't just a point about evolution. These ancient authors thought the heart was where thinking happened (Gen. 6:5; Prov. 23:7; Mark 7:21; Luke 5:22; 24:38; Heb. 4:12). None of them knew about microbes or anything that requires a microscope or telescope to see. That some still find this noteworthy just shows how badly fundamentalism warps people's thinking, getting us to come to these ancient texts with expectations that will inevitably be disappointed. What should be remarkable is how interesting and insightful these authors' writings seem when considered as products of ancient human beings writing within the context of their own time. Saying they were insightful is not a veiled attempt to slip some supernatural significance back in after having removed it. It is a genuine compliment to say this, whereas for fundamentalists saying anything less than "the inerrant word of God" is deemed an insult. Recognizing that these texts are human compositions from millennia ago makes it all the more striking that I still find they speak to me.

Wisdom and Righteousness Outside of Christianity

One learns from studying religion more broadly that insightfulness is not limited to ancient Israel and the early church. As I mentioned in the introduction, the early Christian apologists were aware of this, as were their Jewish precursors such as Philo of Alexandria. Such ancient thinkers were open to learning things from anyone who pursued the truth and diligently sought to understand God and the world. Historically, Christian theologians have been open to insights as long as they were labeled "philosophy" and not "theology." Yet those two categories are not so easily distinguished.* Studying the Bible forced me to rethink what the Bible was and realize that I had much to learn about it as well as from it. Teaching courses about other traditions (and researching those traditions) led me to realize how much I had to learn from a range of voices outside the Christian religion. Whether it was acknowledged or not, your previous version of Christianity had bricks in it that were from elsewhere. Earlier I echoed a phrase from a Greek author who is quoted with approval in the New Testament, but that's far from the only example. Indeed, openness to being surprised by the way those outside your tradition offer something not only positive but even superior is a major theme in the New Testament, albeit one that is often downplayed. See, for instance, Matthew 8:10 // Luke 7:9. Your bricks can come from various places, but if Jesus is the cornerstone, what you've constructed will deserve to be called a form of Christian faith. As you'll see if you compare the versions of this metaphor found in the New Testament (1 Cor. 3:11; Eph. 2:19–21; 1 Pet. 2:1–10), there wasn't agreement among these authors about whether the apostles and other authority figures were part of the foundation or not. There isn't a single unified "biblical" way

* The point has been put wonderfully by Clark Pinnock. See, for instance, his essay "The Finality of Jesus Christ in a World of Religions," in *Christian Faith and Practice in the Modern World*, ed. M. A. Noll and D. F. Wells (Grand Rapids: Eerdmans, 1988), 159, in which he writes, "Why do we look so hopefully to Plato and expect nothing from Buddha? I think we are now entering a period in history when the world religions will begin to impinge on theology as philosophy has always done." See also his *A Wideness in God's Mercy: The Finality of Jesus Christ in a World of Religions* (Grand Rapids: Zondervan, 1992), 133, where he writes, "Theologians in the past did not hesitate to engage Plato and Aristotle in their work. All that is needed is for us to enlarge the circle of conversation partners and include leaders like Buddha and Muhammad in the circle."

of thinking about authority, interpreting scriptural texts, or crafting a worldview. In general, the way I recommend approaching the Bible is by paying more attention to what the biblical authors were doing when they wrote. They were human beings seeking to address pressing concerns in their time, and to do so in a way that gave expression to their faith. The Bible provides an invitation for us to do the same thing in relation to our own time, and to do so in conversation with those who preceded us, including but not limited to the biblical authors.

A whole book could be written just about the various ways biblical scholarship has contributed to my faith in its current form. Let me offer one specific example, what is known as the "new perspective on Paul" (even though it reflects a debate about how to understand Paul's letters that goes back to the ancient church). I remember reading through Galatians for the first time and being baffled by how, after emphasizing so strongly that salvation was not by works, Paul could write in 5:21 concerning the works of the flesh that "those who do such things will not inherit the kingdom of God." Does what we do matter or doesn't it? It was only after reading scholars like James D. G. Dunn and N. T. Wright that the letter began to make sense, and along with it Paul's letter to the Romans.* Rather than being concerned to argue against people trying to earn their way to heaven, the typical Protestant way of understanding Paul, the argument was about works of the law in the sense of Torah, the Jewish law, and thus works that served as identity markers for Jews over against gentiles. Suddenly, Paul's focus on circumcision, food laws, and other such things made sense. Paul wasn't arguing against self-righteousness of an individualistic

* James D. G. Dunn, *The New Perspective on Paul* (Grand Rapids: Eerdmans, 2008); N. T. Wright, *Climax of the Covenant: Christ and the Law in Pauline Theology* (London: T&T Clark, 1993).

sort focused on personal accomplishment, but against a sense of election, of chosenness, that rendered what you do of less importance. By emphasizing special status over righteousness, national belonging became key. Paul was convinced that this stood at odds with the emphasis in the Jewish scriptures themselves that God punishes his people when they rebel, and that God welcomes all people when they seek and obey him. It didn't take long for me to realize that the dominant Protestant interpretation I had heard up until that point made Christians sound less like Paul and more like his opponents! Saying that Christians are saved no matter what they do, while those who are not part of the group are excluded no matter what they do, is almost exactly the stance that Paul was arguing *against*, not for.

I once tried to paraphrase what Paul wrote to the church in Rome in order to see how it would address today's Christians. The recipients of Paul's letters did not think of themselves as Christians over against Jews and gentiles, but as part of the people of God, which they believed could now include gentiles who had been grafted into the children of Abraham (Rom. 11:17–21). Just as we may need to substitute more familiar contemporary figures into Jesus's stories, such as the parables about the man robbed on the Jericho road or the Pharisee and tax collector, to really feel the point being made, it takes putting a word like "Christian" into Romans to feel how Paul's letter sounded to those who thought of the Jews/Israelites as God's people in much the way that many Christians think of themselves. Here's my attempt to paraphrase Romans 2:6–19 to get the message across.

> As Psalm 62:12 says, "God will reward each person according to their deeds." For those who seek glory, honor, and immortality by persisting in doing what is good, there will be eternal life. But for those who act out of self-interest, who disobey the

truth and yield to injustice, there will be passionate anger. There will be suffering and distress for every human being who does evil—first for the Christian, then for the non-Christian. And there will be glory and honor and peace for everyone who does good—first for the Christian, then for the non-Christian. For God shows no favoritism. As many as sin without the Bible will be destroyed without the Bible, and those who have the Bible and sin will be judged in accordance with the Bible. For it is not those who hear the Bible's teachings who are considered righteous before God, but rather those who do what the Bible teaches. For when those who are not Christians and do not have Scripture do by nature what the Bible teaches, they are a Bible for themselves, even though technically they have no Bible. They show that the works taught by the Bible are written on their hearts. Their conscience bears witness to them, and their thoughts will accuse them and/or approve them in the day when God will judge human secrets in accordance with the good news which I proclaim through Jesus Christ.

So you call yourself a Christian, and rely on the Bible, and boast in God, knowing God's will and discerning what really matters because you've received biblical instruction, being confident in your own ability to be a guide to the blind and a light to those in darkness, an educator of the foolish and teacher of the childish, having in the Bible the embodiment of knowledge and truth? Then let me ask you this: Will someone teach others but not also teach themselves? Will you bilk the faithful while preaching "Do not steal"? Will you have affairs while saying "You shall not commit adultery"? If you detest idols, will you commit sacrilege? The one who boasts in the Bible while trampling on the Bible's teaching dishonors God. As the Bible itself says, "Because of you God's name is blasphemed among the nations."

> Being a Christian has value if you put into practice what Jesus taught. But if you disobey his teaching, your belief becomes unbelief. And so if those who are not Christians do the very things that Jesus taught, will not their lack of belief in him be reckoned as belief? The one who is not a Christian and does what Jesus commanded will condemn you who—even though you call yourself a Christian and have the Bible—disobey what is taught therein. For being a Christian is not about outward appearances or the wearing of a particular label (or T-shirts or bumper stickers), but about what happens inwardly, in the secret recesses of the heart, through the Spirit and not mere words. It is not about being applauded by other human beings, but by God.

This attempt at conveying the meaning and the felt impact of Paul's words is rooted in what I have learned from biblical scholarship, and also what I have learned about what is involved in translating biblical and other ancient texts. It is important to have translations that reflect as precise an understanding as possible of their ancient context and their meaning in that time and place. Yet if we do not go beyond that, we risk becoming familiar with ancient peoples and groups such as the Pharisees or Samaritans only as characters in stories whose role and significance we think we know. Making an equivalence even by way of comparison also risks misunderstanding. The Pharisees were not like modern-day fundamentalists, although I've encountered progressive Christians who treat them that way. The Pharisees were a diverse movement that evolved into the rabbinic Judaism of later times. It included individuals like Hillel, who was remembered to have emphasized many of the same things that Jesus did.

Lining up a story's hero with ourselves and a story's villain with our opponents is a sure-fire way to miss the point of one of Jesus's parables. This isn't something that just happens. It is by design. We intentionally do this to feel good about ourselves and avoid being challenged in uncomfortable ways by what the Bible says. In a book like this, it is important to see how the teaching of Jesus and Paul, when understood correctly, challenges rather than supports the views we once held. Recognizing this is crucial to beginning to build a new type of Christian faith that takes our ancient sources more seriously and understands them in a manner informed by scholarship. It is equally crucial to emphasize that if the Bible ever ceases to be heard offering a challenge and critique to my own views and tendencies, present or future, then I am misunderstanding and misusing it just as badly as I did when I was part of conservative evangelicalism. Paul's message in Romans 2 can be paraphrased in other ways, and will need to be, whenever we find ourselves inclined to replace the boundary markers of fundamentalism (not smoking or drinking, or whatever it was in your experience) with new ones (reposting memes and tweets that point out the flaws of fundamentalism, for instance). What I said earlier in the book bears repeating. If you replace your collapsed faith with something equally superficial and merely ideologically opposite, it may be an improvement in some ways, but it won't be the way of Jesus, which calls us to look for the log in our own eye rather than focus on the speck in someone else's (Matt. 7:3–5).

Conclusion

I can understand why you might want to push back against what I've written above. After all, in losing your previous fundamentalism you may feel like you've finally noticed the log that was in your own eye and removed it. Shouldn't I be applauding and encouraging you? I hope this book does indeed do some of that and that what you've read thus far has encouraged you. But anyone who has worked with wood (and especially in an infrequent and amateurish way, like me) will know that getting rid of one splinter doesn't mean you've eliminated them all, much less that you'll be splinter-proof from now on. Following Jesus isn't about finally getting the log out, it is about doing what Jesus said all throughout our journey of faith and the growth and maturation of our views. Keep looking out for logs in your own eye. Keep listening for ways that the Bible helps you recognize your own shortcomings and not only those across the aisle from where you currently align your political and other loyalties. Reading biblical scholarship and theology can help, as again and again you think about what the text meant and what it means. But that alone isn't enough to continue to experience the text speaking to the problems of our time that you are now eager to address. Nor will it make it automatic that you experience the biblical authors' words as a spotlight that helps you notice your own shortcomings and work on growing and improving. Intellectual understanding and exploration of the sort we've focused on in this chapter is crucial. But so too are one's attitude and aims, seeking to integrate scholarly perspectives and information into a multifaceted spiritual and moral journey. In the next chapter we turn to the importance of experience as an aspect of the life of faith, both in the sense of religious experience and also more generally.

Key Points from This Chapter

- Faith is supposed to be trust in God. The desire for certainty is an expression of hubris and leads to idolatry. The appropriate human attitude is to recognize that we are fallible and thus need to trust God.
- Making the Bible into an idol that supposedly provides on God's behalf the certainty we long for is wrong from many perspectives, not least of which is that this has led many to deny

the character of biblical texts as genuinely human writings with all the limitations that entails.

- The Bible reflects the prescientific understanding of its time, and that is not a problem unless you make it one, which you do not have to. Jesus did not call his disciples to reject Greek insights into cosmology or medicine; he called his disciples to love their enemies.
- None of us can know everything. Humbly turning to and relying on the expertise of others can and should become part of your spiritual and intellectual journey.
- Symbols, metaphors, and poetic language can be thought of eucharistically. They point toward a transcendent reality and invite us to encounter that reality, without exhausting it or claiming to do justice to it.
- Whenever we assume that we individually or communally are the correspondents of the "good guys" in biblical stories, we need to examine ourselves and investigate whether that is in fact true.
- God is ultimate reality, and that something is ultimate and exists is certain. There is plenty of room for uncertainty, debate, and exploration about the attributes of God, but none about the existence of God.

For Reflection and Discussion

Do you recognize a fear of uncertainty in yourself? If you try to respond to it not by making yourself feel certain but by letting go and trusting God as the only reality that is ultimate and certain, how does that surrender make you feel? How does letting go of the need for certainty impact your spirituality?

Reflect on a time when you felt certain and later realized with hindsight that you were wrong. How can consideration of such past experiences help you distinguish between being certain and *feeling* certain? What can you learn from that past experience that can guide you going forward?

Take a look at photos related to science (I particularly recommend astronomy photos from NASA). How can you explore them, and the sense of awe and wonder they evoke, in a positive way?

What images and symbols come to mind when you think about God? Why those images? How did you come to associate those images with God? Do they point to ultimate goodness and meaning? If not, what other symbols might be worth exploring? How does it feel to recognize that you have always been responsible for your mental and verbal images of God, even if in the past you accepted those given to you by others?

3

Faith That Experiences

It is both rewarding and challenging to write a book rooted in one's own experience. In the hope that they may be useful to readers, over the course of this book I have shared glimpses of my own journey. It is a story of moving from a faith that was childish to a faith that is childlike. Conservative churches will tell you that having a childlike faith means simply accepting what you are told, believing it without question. I have to ask: Have these people never had children? Children are instinctively curious and inquisitive. If we lose that characteristic as we get into adulthood, it is most likely because our family or church chastened us for constantly asking the most common question children ask: "But *why*?" Growing in maturity in our faith means "putting aside childish things." That means learning to squabble less, to be less prone to shout "mine!" It doesn't mean being less inquisitive. We can be mature and yet keep alive a childlike sense of wonder. Hopefully the previous chapter also helped to make this point unambiguously clear. Just as it takes work to not merely complain about the way things are but instead actively attempt to change them, and just as it takes work not merely to inform ourselves about the Bible and theology but to grapple with the significance of what we learn for our own lives and era, it requires a concerted effort to keep our innate inquisitiveness and sense of wonder about the world alive. I try to do so, and encourage readers to do the same.

This chapter explores experience as a resource for and facet of a mature yet childlike faith. The word "experience" has a variety of connotations. In this chapter I have most or all of them in view:

- Mystical/spiritual experience
- Experience of undeserved suffering as a challenge to our beliefs
- Experience in the sense of the practical knowledge gained through living and working

While this chapter will cover a range of different categories of experience, and ways that those experiences can inform and enrich the life of faith and one's thinking about God, the main unifying theme is experience itself, remaining inquisitive and open to being surprised by things like beauty, and not only by interesting intellectual ideas.

Religious Experience and Mysticism

This is the section of the book that digs deepest into the beginnings and foundation of my own faith, the faith that motivated me to study the Bible at college, only to find that what I learned there challenged things that I had assumed in my spiritual journey up until that point. I suspect that the majority of readers of this book grew up in families and churches where they were indoctrinated with conservative religious ideas. That wasn't my experience. I had a church connection growing up, but it was not of the conservative Protestant variety. In my teens I stopped attending, sensing that there was something missing. This was right after going through the process of confirmation. I thought that afterward I should feel different than I had before, yet I did not. I entered what you might call a seeker phase. At one point I happened across a college radio station that broadcast contemporary Christian music for one hour a week. The songs that I heard there gave expression to a faith and an experience of God that sounded real, unlike my own experience. Not long after, a friend invited me to a concert at her church, and there too the songs expressed a personal experience of God and faith that seemed to be just what I was longing for. I cried, and the following morning at that same church I prayed in a way I hadn't before. I acknowledged that I didn't know what God's way was, but said that whatever it was, I wanted to try it, since my way of living wasn't working. At that moment, a sense of peace came over me. I felt different down to the very core of my being. I surprised my coworkers the following day at work by talking about God. One of them asked me when I had become religious, and I answered honestly: yesterday.

The church where this occurred was a Pentecostal one. If you're familiar with that tradition, it typically puts much more emphasis on experience than on doctrine. On the one hand, the fact that the bedrock of my personal Christian faith was a born-again experience rather than a list of beliefs meant I felt freer to change my mind over the course of my studies than might otherwise have been the case. On the other hand, I shielded that experience from close scrutiny for a long time in much the same manner that fundamentalists typically do with their doctrines. How so? When I shared my story of what I had experienced, some people labeled it "psychological." I was immediately defensive. My experience was real, I insisted, and not "all in my head." In other words, I thought it important to emphasize that what I had experienced was not psychological but spiritual.

Looking back, I now see clearly how misguided such responses were. Of course my experience was psychological. It was an experience! If it didn't involve my brain, it wouldn't be a human experience. I would also presumably have no memory of it if the brain were not involved. Nowadays I have no qualms acknowledging that an experience of this sort depends on and involves our biology, our brain chemistry, firing neurons, and so on. Does that mean that God is "all in my head"? Not necessarily. All human experience involves the brain, not just religious experience. Whether the latter subset of experience involves connection with a transcendent spiritual reality is something I no longer feel the need to try to prove, because how could I ever hope to do so? Instead I prefer to point to the wondrous, puzzling, awe-inspiring, and undeniable reality that we exist in a universe that has given rise to beings like us who have such experiences, and who ponder and debate their significance. Indeed, it is a marvel that there are beings who have experiences of any sort. There is no need to try to "prove" the existence of God through appeal to experience any more than through other arguments. Human experience itself is a sufficient pointer toward that mysterious ultimate Reality.

Having religious experience as a foundation left me open to being shocked and challenged by encounter with other religious traditions. I remember an incident in my teens when I was living overseas and was at the home of a Baptist pastor. Some Latter-day Saints (LDS) missionaries came to the door while I was there, and he invited them in. Like good evangelicals, we saw this as a chance to evangelize *them*. We proceeded to do so, and they reciprocated. In the course of the conversation, one of them presented their reason for accepting the Book of Mormon as scripture alongside the Bible. They said that when they read it, they experienced the Holy Spirit confirming in their heart that it is from God. I didn't voice my reaction out loud, but what I was thinking was, "Hey, that's my line! You're not allowed to say that!" How could someone in a "heretical sect" have an experience like my own? Evangelicals will sometimes claim that when people claim to have an encounter with God or an angel in the context of another religious tradition, it is in fact Satan deceiving that person. That argument is self-defeating. If others could seek God and instead be deceived by demons, the same must be true for me. Those who say, "Ah, but we can rely on the Bible" are just pushing the issue onto others in a way that makes things worse, not better. How could anyone alive today claim to know what spiritual entity if any Paul the apostle or the prophet Muhammad encountered? One thing became clear, when I eventually took a look at the stories about the latter. It made no sense to claim that it was Satan who deceived Muhammad into turning from idols and worshiping the one God of Judaism and Christianity. What would the point of that be? Like so many other things in Christian fundamentalism, this makes no sense when closely examined.

Down the ages, mystical experiences have often opened doors to interreligious dialogue and mutual understanding. When you recognize that the theological language you use to talk about your experience is not a literal descriptor but a pointer to something words cannot adequately grasp or convey, you can potentially view the experience of mystics in other traditions as akin to your own, despite the different symbols and metaphors they use to talk about it.* This is not an argument for saying that all religions are the same. On the contrary, the point is precisely the opposite. Mystics and other open-minded religious people in different religions, who share in common an emphasis on one ultimate Reality that cannot be adequately expressed in words, and who prioritize acting compassionately toward other human beings, may find they have

* While nowadays many people associate India with violence, and there have been examples of that throughout its history, it is also a place where religious traditions have found common ground and fostered mutual acceptance. Let's be honest, the natural way for Muslims to evaluate Hindus is as idolaters. Yet the mystics of India and the Sufi mystics of Islam found points of commonality, sometimes much to the chagrin of the nationalists and the doctrinally focused fundamentalists in both traditions. If you are interested, compare Mughal ruler Akbar's policy on religion to that of his European contemporaries.

more in common with one another than they do with the radical dogmatists and xenophobes in their own tradition. The teaching of Jesus calls us to recognize that the line between good and evil never runs along the border between our group and another, but right through every individual heart and mind, including my own. In the same way, the teaching and example of Jesus call us to be open to recognizing that there might not only be similar faith, but *superior* faith, to be found in people who belong to another tradition. The Gospels tell us that this *surprised* Jesus (Luke 7:1–10 // Matt. 8:5–13). He let himself be surprised, and he learned from it. Following Jesus means being open to being surprised in similar ways.

I'm not sure which presented the bigger challenge for me as someone whose faith was rooted in a personal life-changing experience: being willing to accept that my experience at the very least had psychological aspects to it, or admitting that my experience did not allow me to circumvent historical and doctrinal uncertainty. It is very easy—all too easy—to treat a powerful spiritual experience as confirmation of one's beliefs, the whole package and structure of one's own tradition. The LDS missionary I mentioned did it, and so did I, yet with different sacred texts, churches, and beliefs in view. I also did something similar with doctrines and past events. Eventually I had to recognize that my having an experience of God today does not directly confirm anything about what did or did not happen to a body in a tomb roughly two millennia earlier. Pursuing a spiritual experience in the hope that it might confirm that my beliefs are correct is inherently misguided. It asks an experience to provide what it is incapable of, and the egotism that drives the request is at odds with the goal of spiritual transformation.

Having sought a spiritual "high" in my Pentecostal days, I have become as wary in this area as many readers are in the realm of doctrine. Yet just as theological reflection has a place when we learn to approach it differently than fundamentalists do, so too mysticism ought to have a place even if we view religious experiences differently than we once did. This doesn't mean avoiding experiences that are "merely emotional" but rather recognizing that the emotional and the spiritual cannot be compartmentalized any more than theology can be separated from human intellectual pursuits. The key is to find a balance so that we are not tossed by every wind of sentiment any more than we are tossed about by every wind of doctrine. When you slow down and pay attention, when you look for glimpses of God not apart from the physical reality you inhabit but infused throughout it, you may be surprised not only by what you see but by how you feel, not only in that moment but in your life as a whole.

To be clear, this chapter is not making the case for "reenchantment" of the world, going about expecting angelic apparitions and other things that may have been brought to mind by my discussion. Hopefully the earlier chapters had already made clear that I am not an advocate for rolling back our scientific insights into the world. My point is to not lose some of the richness of what ancient people expressed through language that they took literally and yet which we no longer can. Rudolf Bultmann already expressed the key aspects of this in his writings about demythologization almost a century ago.* His key points were that the Christian gospel is interwoven with an ancient worldview that no leap of faith or imagination can enable a contemporary person to inhabit. Yet it must be possible to translate the message and be authentically Christian in the present. Whatever you make of how he tried to do so, he was not wrong in his analysis of the situation, and he was definitely correct that we cannot just peel off a shell of ancient ideas to reveal a

* See especially Bultmann's essay "New Testament and Mythology," in *Kerygma and Myth: A Theological Debate*, ed. Hans Werner Bartsch (London: SPCK, 1953), 1–44. The book can now be found online at https://www.religion-online.org/book/kerygma-and-myth/.

timeless kernel. We need to understand the meaning of the ancient message in its original context and then figure out what it means to translate it. That, in a sense, is what this book is about, at least for some of its readers. If your prior approach was to try to take things literally, and the collapse of that has just left the rejection of the literal meaning of ancient ideas in its wake, this book asks whether it is possible to find a renewed critical appreciation for the Christian faith, its texts and its concepts, and to find a way to translate them.* I've already done a bit of that throughout the book.

Walter Wink did important work with the concept of spiritual warfare, showing that the elimination of belief in literal demonic entities might cause us to go from not fighting "against flesh and blood" (Eph. 6:12) to fighting against people. While sin is inseparable from people, injustice is institutional and cultural as well as individual. Wink sought to find ways to translate the ancient imagery of spiritual warfare so that it is not reduced to and replaced with an inadequate substitute.** We are meant not to struggle against other individual human beings but against bigger things—systems, tendencies, values, and ideas that hold sway over them. As people of the present day, we resist the temptation to personify them as personal entities deliberately fighting against us. Yet they are no less real and no less serious. This chapter invites you to do the same with your inner spiritual life, to take it seriously while recognizing that you may be struggling against natural instinctive biological urges rather than demonic forces

* See Marcus J. Borg, *Reading the Bible Again for the First Time: Taking the Bible Seriously but Not Literally* (New York: HarperCollins, 2009). See also Paul Ricoeur on second naïveté in *Symbolism of Evil* (Boston: Beacon, 1967), 351–56 (as well as subsequent publications); Paul Tillich on symbols and broken myths in *Dynamics of Faith* (New York: Harper & Row, 1957), 41–54.

** Walter Wink wrote a series of books on this topic. See perhaps most conveniently *The Powers That Be: Theology for a New Millennium* (New York: Doubleday/Random House, 1998).

attacking you from outside. There is more than one way to do this, to update the language used to express spiritual struggle within oneself as well as outwardly with societal trends and structures. What I offer here is not a one-size-fits-all program but an encouragement to explore ways to translate the old for your time and context so that deconstruction does not result in the loss of the richness of what mysticism and spirituality can offer even to people in our day and age.

Music and Mysticism

Those who had a bad experience with dogmatism may forever be wary of doctrinal claims. And those who become aware of how easy it is to mistake our own inner voice or our own emotions for a message from God may be forever wary about mysticism. In my case, I make a concerted effort not to let past negative experiences, and thinking critically about what I previously accepted without question, rob me of things that can enrich my life. I encourage you to do likewise, to learn balance. This is true in everything we've covered thus far. Whether it is skepticism or openness, flexibility or steadfastness, what is potentially a good thing becomes something unhealthy and unhelpful when taken to an extreme. Often those who analyze the biblical text, or music, find it hard thereafter to enjoy simply experiencing it. If creating an emotional high through music is something you consider a means of manipulation, you might view any religious music—or any music at all—with suspicion. I could easily have ended up feeling the same way. But music is too meaningful, in too many ways, for me to eliminate it from my life. My life would be impoverished without music. I can put on music that moves me and enjoy being moved by it. I look forward to the experience, the glimpse of transcendence it provides.

The fact that an experience is emotional and involves our brain chemistry need not rob it of its personal spiritual significance for us. Think about love between human beings as an analogy. Must recognition of the involvement of hormones and brain chemistry in romantic love rob us of the experience of connecting with and spending our lives with someone? If we treat analysis and understanding as antithetical to experience and enjoyment, our lives end up impoverished. They call this mistaken way of thinking about scientific explanation *reductionism* for a reason. The fact that you can study and understand the processes at work when the taste receptors in your tongue enjoy a really good cup of coffee, and in your brain as the caffeine does its work, is no reason to forgo the experience. (If you aren't persuaded, try rereading this paragraph first thing in the morning—without coffee.) Things like romantic attachment and enjoyment of flavors can lead us in unhealthy and ultimately self-destructive directions. It is just as important and necessary to understand and acknowledge this as it is to not allow the need for caution to keep us from finding a significant other or enjoying delicious food. It is possible to find a healthy balance between letting ourselves experience life and thinking critically about our experiences. It is crucially important to work toward doing so, and to try to turn this difficult balancing act into a good habit that begins to come naturally.

In conservative Christian music, the lyrics are the focus. For me now, it is the beauty of music itself that provides the most helpful pointer to God. Not all of the music I enjoy is without words. However, the music with lyrics that moves me nowadays is more likely to be a choral work by a twentieth-century British composer than a song by a twentieth- or twenty-first-century writer of praise music. That has as much to do with the music itself and how I connect with it as with the words. If that music is completely unfamiliar to you, I don't recommend jumping straight from contemporary Christian music to choral works by Herbert Howells, Charles Villiers Stanford, and Hubert Parry (although by all means give them a listen if you're so inclined). That's for the same reason I wouldn't recommend jumping straight to some of my favorite orchestral works. My musical tastes evolved slowly. Cultivating musical appreciation is a lot like cultivating appreciation of a more diverse array of foods. Your first impression of Indian food may be that it is "spicy." You may or may not like it. If you keep eating it, trying different dishes, you will likely be able to single out which ones have cardamon, cloves, and cinnamon, which ones have fenugreek, and so on. In the same way, listening to more elaborate music or exploring more complex philosophical and theological ideas almost always involves a process, a first taste and initial impression that make you either avoid repeating the experience or wanting to try a little more. Soon you want to try something different within the same category, and before you know it you're recognizing individual ingredients, perceiving schools of thought, and you can be much more specific about what kind of music moves you than to just say "classical" or "jazz." If you have become accustomed to spicy food, you hopefully know to tone down the heat when ordering for a friend who is trying that type of food for the first time. The same applies to music, and to theology (some of which is quite spicy).

Music provided an illustration of things we focused on in earlier chapters. Here, however, my focus is mainly on letting yourself simply *experience* all of these things. When theology is about conveying definitive truth, when eating is about ceasing to be hungry, and when songs are about saying something through the lyrics, there may be little room for slowing down and just savoring. Cultivating this slow, appreciative approach to life in general isn't something new. It is there in the Bible's wisdom traditions, including much of the teaching of Jesus.* Noticing the lilies of the

* It is also to be found in the Christian tradition, in practices like *lectio*

field, paying attention to them, thinking about them, and expecting to learn something by doing so presuppose that our experiences shape our religious views and that the natural world can serve as a teacher (Matt. 6:28 // Luke 12:27). As we saw above, noticing the different ways a musical performance can be described helped me think about subjects like materialism, scientific reductionism, and the relationship between God and the universe. I didn't turn to music expecting it to do those things. Indeed, if I had listened to music with the exclusive aim of finding in it an illustration of a theological point, I am certain I would not have enjoyed the music as much, and thus would not have made the analogies that I did. When we approach a text or life in general looking for something very specific, that focus may keep us from noticing so much else that is there, valuable things we weren't even aware we needed.

Teaching at a university, I have wrestled with how to ensure that students do reading, and that they do it in helpful ways. Quizzing them on the names of characters and plot points risks conveying that they should be memorizing details when reading a novel, simply to get a good grade on a quiz. I have therefore moved away from giving these sorts of quizzes, because the point of reading a novel is to *experience* it. The same is true with biblical and all other literature, with music, and ultimately with life as a whole. When we take this approach, living in and savoring the moment, we notice beauty in ways that many of the authors of Psalms, proverbs, and parables in the Bible also clearly did.

Transitioning from reading to pass a quiz to reading for pleasure can take time. Reading for transformation can be viewed as

---

divina in the Western church and the Jesus prayer in the Eastern churches. The key point is less about which of these you explore (and it may potentially be both) and more about doing something along these lines, slowing down and paying close attention to biblical material in a manner that engages the mind but is not exclusively intellectual.

another level beyond that. Neither enjoyment nor transformation can be demanded from literature. Some works won't provide such an experience no matter how you approach them. Even those with the potential to do so will not do so in the same way for everyone. The same is true of novels, of music, and of the varied texts that make up the anthology we call the Bible. If you got used to reading the Bible looking for additional data points for your systematic theology, or prooftexts to use in your Internet debates with infidels, then reading it to be surprised by the experience may be difficult. I mention that with some trepidation, since reading with the aim of having a transformative experience in mind may prevent it from happening. Just read. Just listen.

Try new theologians and scholars who've written on this or that subject. Never forget your own process of deepening your experience. I hope that once you've rebuilt your worldview you will invite and assist others who want to do likewise. But your favorite author may be unpalatable to someone who hasn't followed the same path as you, or who is on the same path but not at the same point on the path. Remember where you started, which next steps you took, and recommend those, and you may avoid viewing those who disagree with you with disdain. If you've read this book up until this point, there is a reasonable chance that you held different views in the past than you do now. You may have been a lot like your friends and family members who are now trying to persuade you how wrong and misguided you are. You didn't get where you are all at once, even if some specific text or experience played a decisive role at a crucial moment. It is easy to want to forget how you used to view the world. It is tempting to say that you were once a fool and now are wise. A lot of fundamentalists are extremely clever people. It takes an agile mind to maintain a worldview at odds with so much of what the Bible, the natural world, and society show to be the case. If you hold more healthy views now, remember the process that brought this about. Cultivate compassion and empathy, especially toward those who hold the views you once held. If your new worldview is more scientifically and biblically accurate, but isn't also kind and loving, it isn't Christian and isn't moral.

The Experience of Suffering

Pete Enns has written a whole book on the curveballs in life and the need to be open to experiences that change our direction and our perspective.* That includes unpleasant experiences. Reflecting on how we respond to our own suffering and that of others is crucial to the moral and spiritual life of any human being, and not only for Christians. It is not only a question of how we make intellectual sense of the world in light of this aspect of it. There is also the attitudinal question that must not be neglected. Will we become bitter, cynical, and chagrined? Or will we let the unkindness of others motivate us to view kindness as all the more important, and make that much more concerted an effort to be kind ourselves?

Fundamentalists are notorious for denouncing and denigrating those who allow their theologies to be influenced by experience. Ironically, the Bible that they say ought to be the sole authority to the exclusion of experience actually emphasizes the importance of changing our minds in light of experience! Probably the best and clearest example of this is the book of Job. Many people think the book is about the problem of evil, offering an explanation of why bad things happen to good people. There are, however, difficulties with that view. To begin with, Job is never told why he suffered. Even if he had been, it is hard to imagine he would have taken comfort from

* Peter Enns, *Curveball: When Your Faith Takes Turns You Never Saw Coming (or How I Stumbled and Tripped My Way to Finding a Bigger God)* (New York: HarperCollins, 2023).

what the book's prologue reveals to the reader. Job is especially righteous, and for this reason he is singled out for attention in a discussion among the sons of God. A figure referred to as the Accuser is sometimes mistaken for the later notion of a fallen angel named Satan. "Satan" does mean accuser in Hebrew. The figure in Job, however, is a full-fledged member of the celestial court of the sons of God with the title "the Accuser." He acts only by the authority granted to him, and the questions he raises in his role as the heavenly "prosecuting attorney" are important and valid ones. There is a good reason why Job is so righteous—he is paid well for being righteous (Job 1:9–11). If he has to be a good person without being rewarded for it, then and only then will it be possible to tell whether he is indeed genuinely good or not. So a bet is made between the deity whom Job worships and the Accuser. If you were Job, and were told that your children died, your property was destroyed, and you were afflicted with shingles so that God could win a bet about you, would it make you feel better or worse about your suffering? The main point of the book seems rather to be the question raised by the Accuser. If the world were made in such a way that everyone consistently got what they deserved, it would undermine genuine goodness, giving us selfish motives for what would otherwise be selfless acts.

Another major point is made through the way Job responds to his friends. Job's conversation partners insist that Job and his children must have done something to deserve their misfortune. Job tells his friends that he once thought as they did, but he knows that he has not done anything that justifies his intense suffering. He would take God to court to prove it if he could. When God appears at the end of the book, some think it is in order to bully Job into submission. "Sit down and shut up! You know nothing! Who do you think you are?" The problem with that interpretation is that at the end, God is said to be pleased with Job for having spoken rightly about God when his friends did not (Job 42:7).

That is another major point of the book. It is better to complain honestly than to set yourself up as defender of God's reputation. God is great enough to not need you to safeguard God's honor. Job's friends were not defending God, they were defending their understanding of God and of how the world worked. They were trying to avoid deconstruction. They were willing to lie about Job, about the way the world works, and ultimately about God in their effort to avoid rethinking their worldview. Job on the other hand plowed courageously ahead. As a result, he as a character and we as readers of this tale have a story that encourages us to allow our experiences to shatter our theological boxes. Losing the security of our tidy equations about God and the workings of the universe is an experience that leads us into wider theological pastures. Our new ways of thinking still cannot hold or do justice to God, but at least they don't reduce and misrepresent God quite so badly. In the context of this chapter, note that Job seems satisfied at the end of the book not because he has an answer to the question of why he suffered, nor an argument for divine justice, but because he had an encounter with God. I suspect that if you continue your pursuit of God and have a transformative religious experience, your unanswered questions will remain and yet will pale in significance in the light of that life-changing encounter.

Conclusion

This chapter is intentionally shorter than those that preceded it. It would have felt distinctly odd to write at greater length about the subject of experience. Better to end this chapter slightly more quickly, and leave you a bit of extra time to put on some music. What will be meaningful to you depends a lot on what you've listened to before. If you'd like recommendations, I regularly share links to YouTube videos on social media of music I find meaningful and inspiring. My main recommendation is not that you listen to any specific works, but that you take time to actually listen, rather than just putting music on in the background while doing something else. By all means keep doing that as well if you're so inclined. But on occasion take the time to genuinely listen. This doesn't mean trying to force your mind not to wander, or trying not to think about anything (as though that were actually possible). Listen, and let your thoughts wander where they will. You may even end up having a much-needed nap. That too can make a positive contribution to one's spiritual life. When we imagine the spiritual as divorced from or even antithetical to the body, we do an injustice to our minds and our bodies, which ultimately are simply aspects of our whole selves. If you are trying to work on cultivating a deeper experience of God and a kinder and more moral behavior, yet don't sleep enough, you'll likely be irritable and unfocused.

Also make time (and if it feels unnatural to do so, then make the effort) to talk to God. When we lose the sense of God as an anthropomorphic entity, we may lose any expectation that we might hear God's voice or that it makes sense to assemble our own words into prayers. For the postfundamentalist or the post-Pentecostal, that may be a positive and necessary step, at least initially. It is common for those with a simplistic and dogmatic faith to try to make their spiritual lives conform to a particular way of reading Scripture's stories, expecting to hear God providing constant commentary on and input into their lives as they imagine was true for Abraham and Moses and others. You might not have expected it to come in audible verbal form, but there was the expectation that God was constantly telling you things through circumstances or how you felt. If that was how you thought about prayer, you may have needed to take a break for a bit. But if you're reading this book (which is not just about refraining from problematic things you used to do but doing different and better things instead, creating new positive habits), then you're likely ready to move on. When we cut that inner dialogue that characterizes prayer out of our spiritual lives entirely and for good, we stop exploring our inner selves. Whether the insights that come in response to such exploration come from God or the depths of our subconscious is unanswerable. That question poses a false antithesis, as though the infinite God does not encompass our psyches along with everything else.

The fundamentalist Christian demand that its specific brand of Christianity offer something inherently different from and superior to what anyone else does is born of prideful competitiveness. Historically, Christians have recognized that God is found by those who seek God no matter their religious background or people group (Acts 10:34–35; 17:27). Instead of demanding a way of pursuing God that offers certainty, that bypasses the subjectivity of your own human psychology, it is better to explore your innermost depths as well as the farthest distances our telescopes allow us to glimpse. It is at the edges of what we can see, or what we can know, of what we can express in words, that people throughout recorded history have found (or been found by) a life-transforming encounter with God.*

To be clear, being humble and not consigning others to hell does not mean "everything goes," that you become one of those wishy-washy people who says that everyone's way is equal and

* Karl Rahner was in the habit of saying that the Christian of the future will be a mystic, someone who has had a personal experience of God, or will not exist at all. See his "Christian Living Formerly and Today," in *Theological Investigations*, vol. 7 (New York: Herder & Herder, 1971), 15. Note also my favorite quote from the Sufi mystic Rabi'a of Basra, in which she asks God to throw her into hell if she worships God out of fear of hell. Her prayer is that, if she worships God simply for its own sake, because God is worthy, she will be allowed a glimpse of God's beauty. That is my prayer for readers of this book as well.

good, and we should all just agree to disagree. We can do better than that. I am always dismayed when students in my classes make it sound as though these big questions are matters of such complete uncertainty that we may as well not bother, as though there is nothing to be gained from thinking about them, as though they are ultimately trivial. The topics discussed or in the background throughout this book relate to our highest aspirations, our deepest fears, and our most central values. Seeking the right way to live, and the best way of speaking about God, benefits from and indeed requires that we be prepared to discuss and to disagree. The difference from what one finds in fundamentalism is this: We should not be quick to assume that we are right. We should have convictions, and humility, and maintain a creative and vibrant tension between the two. Or to put it another way, one of our convictions should be that we can be wrong, that we have things to learn from others, and that it is therefore in the best interest of both us and others to approach our conversations accordingly.

Key Points from This Chapter

- Unusual emotional and cognitive experiences have played a role in human history, interpreted as pointers to truths beyond what we normally perceive in our everyday lives.
- The experience of suffering leads some to cling to religious beliefs and others to shift them. The book of Job and other texts in the Bible provide positive examples of both types of responses.
- Allow room for your own inner voice to engage in conversation, even if at this point you might not label it as prayer or believe that it is indeed a conversation with a divine other. The practice itself can be meaningful.
- Listen to instrumental music from the present and the past, in different genres. Just listen attentively rather than multitasking,

and let your mind and thoughts go wherever they will. If you play an instrument, explore improvisation.

- Go for walks or bike rides. Be on the lookout for and notice beauty.

For Reflection and Discussion

Start keeping a journal.

What positive religious and spiritual experiences have you had in the past? What is their significance to you now? How might such experiences be understood as part of the new worldview that you are building?

Reflect on a particularly low point in your life. What religious significance did you attribute to it at the time? Do you view it differently now?

Think about a time when your experience was at odds with your beliefs, and you clung to them nonetheless. Do you still think you responded in the best way to your experience? What might you have learned at the time if you had been more open to changing your ideas? How can you become more open to learning from experience in the future?

4

Faith That Connects

Let me begin this last chapter with a question that perhaps I ought to have asked earlier. As you have been reading this book, did you talk about its contents, or your feelings about the book, with anyone else? Was it discussion online? In-person over coffee? Was it at home with members of your family? All, some, or none of the above? I ask this not to elicit a particular answer to the question, much less to make you feel guilty for your answer, but simply as a natural way to move from what has preceded into this last chapter. Depending on your experience, going to church may have been an obligation you are glad to be rid of (Heb. 10:25), or it may be the one thing you miss most from your faith in its previous form. Some experience worldview collapse because they feel betrayed by a leader or a community they thought was trustworthy and loving but which proved to be anything but. Others experience a collapse of their intellectual belief system and stop meeting with those who still hold their old views, even though they miss dearly the sense of community and camaraderie.

The important thing is that, whether your experience was a positive one or a negative one (or a bit of both), the good and bad of church community is a reflection of what happens when human beings congregate and collaborate. Some churches promise that Christian community is different from what you will find anywhere else. Others are more honest, emphasizing that it should be different as a goal to strive for, yet acknowledging that we regularly fall short. Most goals are ones that we will at times slip up on. But if we do not make the effort at all, we will be in a much worse situation than if we try and fail. The person who doesn't bother trying to eat healthy food, and the person who does so almost always but occasionally makes exceptions, will be worlds apart as far as their well-being is concerned. The same applies to the effort to be a loving community. As human beings we hunger for community.* Whether you prefer to say we are made for it or we evolved for it, the need for it is woven into our biology and our psychology at deep levels. Other types of living organisms can survive on their own as soon as they are born. Not so humans. We are dependent on others from the start and for years afterward. We can manage on our own for periods of time (and we introverts are in general happier to do so than others), but no one is happy in a situation of ongoing isolation.

Perhaps there was no need for this introduction, but I suspected that some readers might need that little bit of extra convincing that this chapter is for them, that it is worthwhile trying the community thing again after having been wounded in the past. Hopefully those hungering for community will take the lead and create communities that do a better job of being supportive and caring while embracing and not merely tolerating diversity. Do it not just for yourselves but also for the benefit of others who are too burdened and jaded to take the initiative on this, or never had good models to emulate and adapt from. In every area this book has covered, some will take the lead and be eager to pursue that aspect of the Christian life. Others will recognize that certain things are not their focus or their forte, but that doesn't mean they want

* An important article on the decline of church attendance, and the irony that it happens at a time when people feel increasingly lonely and isolated, is Jake Meador, "The Misunderstood Reason Millions of Americans Stopped Going to Church," *Atlantic*, July 29, 2023, https://tinyurl.com/2m7uvp7f.

to forgo those things altogether. When you rebuild your intellectual worldview, it may seem that it is a purely private matter. But as your views impact how you live, and as you work on creating community, others benefit besides you.

I'll get into a lot of the details in the remainder of the chapter. The central points, however, can be made very succinctly. First and foremost: Find your people. If they aren't where you are, find them online. Even then, don't settle just for long-distance networking, even though that can be rich and rewarding. Build community where it isn't present, locally as well as globally. Even if the majority in your immediate vicinity are antagonistic to your effort to be part of an open, reconstructed, well-informed, and diverse Christian community, it is extremely unlikely that you are completely alone. There are often many others who are too scared of being shunned by family and other loved ones to ever say they are longing for something different. You may have been such a person for a time. You were not and are not the only one. Your bravery in what you have done so far and what you will soon do has the potential to inspire, encourage, and assist others.

Second, if you are already meeting regularly with others to talk about theology, collaborate for social change, or do things related to your faith, then you are still "doing church," as some would say. You may not be "going to church" in the traditional sense of gathering on Sunday morning in a building called a "church." When Christianity first began, there was no such building, no designated day to gather, no set time, no set program. And there is no requirement for what church will look like in the future. I emphasize this because, if you are an introvert like me, the idea of starting the process of connecting with people and making friends can be particularly daunting. What has been true in every chapter is also true here. There are steps that are still ahead of you (there always were and always will be), but there are also important steps you've already taken. Whether deconstruction is a slow and steady process or one that seems sudden and catastrophic, it teaches us important lessons. Even before you began reading this book, you had come a long way and had acquired a lot of resources that will be useful to you. Sometimes we need someone to come along and provide us with resources we lack, but in many instances what we need is for someone to come along and help us learn to use things we already have in new ways.

Back to Basics

If I had called this section "Back to the Bible," you would have thought it sounded worryingly like a fundamentalist slogan. Yet in a faith that recognizes that the early church was a group of human beings working together (and sometimes in tension with one another) to figure out what their movement should be like, it is still good to go back to the Bible. Doing so does not have to represent a deferral to an authority. Instead, it can be a recognition that being a Christian today means engaging our heritage in conversation even if we end up doing something different than past Christians did. There is continuity to be maintained in creative tension with our efforts to contextualize and be relevant. Not everything old is bad, just as not every innovation is an improvement. Looking at what the early church did often makes clear to us as nothing else can that there are other options besides those we have experienced. That is true no matter what kind of church you or I may have attended. Nothing done in our time is precisely what the early church did.

Knowing the practices of the early church doesn't in any way obligate us to imitate them precisely or indeed at all. You surely have noticed that selling all one's belongings and practicing a sort of "love communism" is not a typical practice in so-called Bible-believing churches despite the descriptions of this in Acts. Fundamentalists pick and choose, and you're free to do so too. We can only ever maintain partial and selective continuity with the past. The issue with fundamentalists is that they deny they are doing this. Sometimes the continuity is a superficial one or even a mere façade. Applying a label derived from the Bible to our practices does not mean that we are genuinely doing the same things as the early Christians, or that if we are imitating them, our actions have the same significance for us as theirs did for them. When we recognize that the New Testament writings are human creations, we can be open to evaluating and departing from approaches they came up with, as well as remain open to their practices that will probably always make sense for human beings who share values and goals. There is no need to reinvent the wheel. The most unhelpful thing that someone who has left a tradition can do is to refuse to believe or do anything that they previously did, assuming that it was all wrong. Just as no human individual or community gets everything right, none of us is entirely and completely wrong about everything.

References in the book of Acts about followers of the Way "breaking bread" probably call to mind communion, the Lord's Supper, something liturgical. That may indeed have been part of it, as is suggested in 1 Corinthians 11. But Acts and Paul's letters reveal that the phrase's primary significance was its everyday meaning as a Greek phrase. They ate meals together. In other words, the earliest followers of Jesus did a lot of what we'd call "hanging out." Meals were (and to some extent today still are, in many cultures) the primary occasion for that happening. The impression we get in Acts 20 is that they got together to share a meal and spent time in educational conversation beforehand. While the custom of the Greek symposium after dinner provided a context in which some philosophers taught, that practice was often restricted to men. Between the gender inequity as to who was included and the inequity of who could afford to stay late given their disparate economic statuses and work schedules, the early Christians may have chosen to move the teaching to before dinner. Paul's criticism of the church in Corinth in 1 Corinthians 11 may reflect their doing what was the norm in their society rather than what he felt should characterize Christians. It sounds as though the wealthy hosts and their friends dined before those who came from work were even able to arrive. The latecomers then had to stay hungry until the after-teaching meal was served to them.

The difference between translations as to what Paul did before and after the meal in Acts 20 is very interesting. Some translations say he preached or taught, but the Greek words used in Acts 20:7–8, 11 more naturally indicate that Paul *conversed* with the gathered believers in Troas.* We should not play this off against teaching, since the best teachers teach in an interactive way. There could be long speeches and lectures, to be sure, but there was at the very least room for questions and discussion. Some, like Socrates, became famous for teaching in a freer conversational manner. I may be biased, but I am inclined to think that this part of church activity in those days was more like what happens in my adult Sunday school class than what we think of as a typical sermon nowadays. There was discussion, with everyone involved learning from everyone else.

The summary of what their gatherings were typically like in Acts 2:42 shows that fellowship was a priority, listed even before

* C. K. Barrett comments on the word used in 20:7–8: "The meaning varies between dialogue, discussion between two or more persons, and discussion in which one person discusses a matter, as in a sermon or lecture" (*Acts, Volume 2: 15–28*, International Critical Commentary [London: T&T Clark, 2004], 951). The word in verse 11 means to socialize and talk with one another rather than to preach in the modern monodirectional way, as its occurrence in Luke 24:14 makes clear.

prayer, and integral to pretty much everything on the list, so that its inclusion as a separate point serves to highlight its centrality rather than diminish it to merely one item among many. They came together to hang out in the setting it was natural to do so, namely, meals, and in that context they learned and prayed but, as Acts emphasizes, the act of fellowship, of hanging out, was important in its own right.

In the first century, those associated with the Jesus movement gathered on Sunday after work. It wasn't a day off at that time. The symbolism of that day—the first day of the week being the day on which Jesus had risen from the dead—led them to meet on that day whenever they could. It was the day after the Sabbath (i.e., Saturday), and so Jewish members of the community had had an opportunity to rest, which others in this movement did not. When Christianity became the dominant religion in various societies, the weekend was extended to include Sunday so that people would be free to attend church. Nowadays, many people think of Sundays as days off that can and should be utilized for sporting and other events. There is, to be sure, an irony about how things developed. A day that was kept free in order to make it possible to go to church is now widely utilized for things that take priority over going to church. The response should not be to complain and berate people for not refusing to have their kids play sports and do other things that their peers are doing. Sunday mornings have become a less convenient time for churches to gather, but for the earliest Christians Sunday morning wasn't even an option. That was a workday. The custom has changed before and can change again. There is nothing "biblical" about churches meeting on Sunday mornings. Perhaps it is time to reconsider gathering in evenings or on other days of the week, as well as in other venues. (My current Sunday school class began as a weekday house group but shifted to Sunday mornings before church because finding a weekday evening that worked consistently for everyone proved impossible. The point is not that weekday evenings are better, or that Sunday mornings are. The point is that having a time set aside when an entire society is free to gather is a luxury that we take for granted that was not part of early Christian experience.)

One group that I was involved in starting in my student days emerged naturally from regular get-togethers among PhD students. It turned out that others were interested in hanging out and discussing the Bible and theology too. We called ourselves "House to House," taking a phrase and our model from the book of Acts (Acts 2:46; 5:42). Taking turns gathering at different homes may work for you. So might meeting at a pub and having a beer while chatting about the Bible, theology, your efforts to address local injustices, or anything else. Conversations while playing sports or board games, or while you offer a meal to the needy in your community, are also good or might even become the dominant model. In the past, getting people together to hear an individual who had studied as Paul had was the only way to let everyone benefit from such learning. Today you can hear excellent talks on YouTube and get immediate access to serious books in electronic form either through your local library or by purchasing them. Our need to get together with other people has not changed, but the older rationales for doing so no longer apply. It may be that the church needs to adapt, just as it always has. Adaptation hasn't happened everywhere at the same pace, and sometimes churches have failed and fallen as a result. This should not be used to shame or judge any individual congregation or denomination. As many have ruined things by innovating in ways that jumped on a bandwagon that went nowhere, as have failed to sense where the Spirit was moving and to turn in that direction. This is the crucial point. There is no source ancient or contemporary that will provide us with a particular way of "doing church" that is guaranteed to work for a particular context, and to prove successful in the long term. Don't try to guess. Try to meet needs. Begin with your own, which you perhaps know best. Start there, but don't end there. Be flexible enough to be about more than the one thing you consider most important. Try new things and see where they go. The early church did so, and what they pioneered is still going, even if it looks very different. I am certain that if they could see into our time, they'd be dismayed by some of what is being done that claims to be church and delighted by other things.*

Finding (or If Necessary, Creating) Your People

When you are a *Star Trek* fan, or a Dungeons & Dragons player, or other variety of geek, and you suddenly discover others with similar interests in your workplace or school or neighborhood, there is a reasonable chance that you may say you "found your people." When it comes to religion, however, it isn't always immediately obvious who "your people" are. Many people think of the "nones" and others who have stopped attending church as people who have abandoned Christianity or are done with religion altogether. For some of them this is the case, but by no means all. Nones are the whole gamut of people who no longer check the traditional boxes on the census or questionnaire. This does not necessarily mean they have abandoned belief in God or Jesus, although some have. Many have simply stopped going to church. If you have any connection with Christianity, you'll know that attendance has been declining. We've pointed out some of the main reasons throughout this book and earlier in this chapter. Some no longer identify with

* Since there are no time machines, I cannot prove this to you, but neither can you prove me wrong. For a short story about time machines and faith, see my story "Certainty," first published in my book *Theology and Science Fiction*.

the beliefs preached from the pulpit. Others don't see any reason to go hear sermons in a local venue when a selection of the best sermons ever preached is readily available online. We can list many reasons. Some would say one of these things was the reason they stopped going, while a few might say all of them were. Here I'd like to point out the irony that, as Christian church attendance is in decline everywhere, atheist churches have been popping up. People who used to go to church are happy to be rid of much of it but consistently miss the sense of community. If many atheists find church necessary, there is a lesson in this. A lot of people who are fed up with what they previously experienced still hunger for something. Think about the many "spiritual but not religious" people who are happy to try out lots of things that are in fact religious, as long as they are not from the particular tradition they came from and have come to find disappointing. Some "nones" are still searching, and some have shifted to another viewpoint that they think provides what their previous one didn't. All of us need to connect with other people, and need some of them to share core values so that we can provide mutual encouragement as well as be challenged and held accountable. Whether one looks at Christians, atheists, or any other group, it is typically those who think they need no one else that introduce toxicity into the constituency. If you think that by moving to a different community you're going to escape this human trait, I have bad news for you. You may have had a bad experience in Christian circles, but there isn't another group where you are guaranteed not to have the same kind of experience. Approaching community realistically, and working to make whatever community you find or create a good one, is the best you can do.

If all human beings long to find their people, don't exempt yourself, pretending that you don't need anyone. But as you look for or seek to create community, what form should that take? Reconstructing one's own faith is challenging enough. Am I now really asking you to reconstruct a whole community? I suppose on one level I am, but I need to clarify in what sense. Lots of people are on the same journey you are and at the same stage. Just to be clear, that doesn't mean they think like you. If you experienced the negative impact of a demand for conformity in your past religious affiliation, hopefully you won't try to replicate it in the future. Being an intolerant fundamentalist at the other end of the ideological spectrum should never be the aim. Find a group that is mutually committed to seeking God and following Jesus, one that recognizes that what that means may differ from one person to the next.

Unity in fundamentalism is achieved by policing borders and multiplying boundary markers. If Jesus said that anyone who is not against us is for us (Mark 9:40), then he advocated a different sort of unity, one that has a minimal core, a focal point and anchor, as what provides a unifying center. In mathematical and sociological terms, it is the difference between a bounded set and a centered set. Your group may not be the right fit for someone who really doesn't like Jesus as they perceive him. You should be okay with that, just as you would be okay with someone not attending who doesn't think you should welcome and include all the different sorts of people that you do in your community. Returning to the saying of Jesus we quoted, you will also find yourself creating relationships with other individuals and groups who do not see eye to eye with you, and respect you despite differences. That is what Jesus was talking about in Mark 9:38–41. The disciples thought that an exorcist who was invoking Jesus's name should be stopped. Jesus told them to view him not as a competitor but as a potential ally.

Being inclusive is compatible with setting boundaries. That isn't a paradox. If the majority of a community are seeking to foster love, the presence of hateful people who refuse to set aside their hatred will pull in the opposite direction. The tensions will at best distract from your goal and at worst tear the community apart. Everyone has multiple commitments and values, and because they end up in tension with one another, we must regularly choose which to prioritize, both as individuals and as communities. Decide in advance and you'll avoid controversy. Do you really want to be a forum for free speech where no idea is excluded, or do you want to be a welcoming place and prohibit expressions of bigotry and hate speech? In theory it might be great to hold to both equally, and both are indeed good things in the abstract. Eventually situations arise in which commitment to one conflicts with commitment to the other. Choose from the outset which you prioritize and you may still be criticized for your choice, but not in the way you will be for inconsistency later on if you didn't address the topic up front.

Having defined your core commitment(s) that can unify, strive to be as open as possible to those who are different. Don't ever surround yourself *only* with people who think the way you do now. If you were previously in an ideological bubble, avoid that pitfall this time around. It is difficult to avoid self-deception and self-righteousness when we surround ourselves with people who will only applaud whatever we do and never disagree with us or challenge us. This isn't an easy thing to accomplish, nor an easy thing to maintain, despite being so important and worthwhile. It is no wonder that even in diverse denominations, most individual congregations fall somewhere along the ideological spectrum, catering to a particular kind of musical preference, particular theological views, and so on. After all, Murphy's Law says that if you try to please everyone, no one will like it. A church should not be trying to please everyone. As an educator, I recognize that different people learn differently, that introverts may not be as vocal participants in class discussion as extroverts are. It isn't an attempt to please everyone if I set up my grading system to reward different kinds of participation. It is an attempt to be fair and inclusive.

A church that welcomes people of diverse musical tastes needs to offer a means for them to connect to God each in their own way. In doing so, the church won't make everyone happy, and will make some people distinctly unhappy. In other contexts, that might be a worrying thing. If, however, our aim is spiritual and moral growth, then we need the experience of a community in which we take delight when the needs of others are being met at the expense of our own. In short, you want to find or create your people, and your people should ideally be a group committed to inclusivity and to the good of everyone. In an era when relationships are discarded when they do anything other than make us happy, this will be distinctly countercultural, in a way that it ought to be.

It can be a struggle to maintain the sense of community while members are at different points in their journeys of faith. That is why so many churches of every perspective settle for a least-common-denominator approach that assumes everyone is forever locked at the kindergarten Sunday school level. This is not something new nor something unique to Christianity or even to religion. It doesn't have to be that way. If what unites a group is a commitment to following Jesus, then it is possible for people with different understandings of what that means to respect that each person is nonetheless on a shared journey. Each may consider the other to be the one who is lagging behind. That too is nothing new (see Rom. 14).

Often communities settle into ways of doing things that no one considers satisfactory, and yet things never seem to change, not because alternatives are unimaginable or impossible but because they are difficult to institute. The remedy to a disappointing experience with community is not to give up on community and acknowledge defeat, but to strive for better community. A rewarding experience of community does not always happen even when we invest time and effort, but it will never happen without us doing our best and working for the good of all.

Is This Church?

Just because your gathering isn't like any past iteration of Christian community doesn't mean you can't call it a church. Indeed, it might be a good reason *to* call it one. The Greek term in the Gospels simply means an assembly, a gathering of people. The Greek word that gives us the English term "synagogue" basically means the same thing. There were all kinds of assemblies in the era in which Christianity arose. A couple of terms for gatherings over time became names for specific types of gatherings, and then eventually became names for the buildings in which those groups met. Perhaps we should say that church is what Christians do. Ultimately you should call it whatever you find helpful. Some are put off by the term "church" because of past experience. If that is your case, substitute something else. There is no need to use a label that describes your way of being or doing church, either. The early disciples' references to their assembly didn't communicate what kind of assembly it was to those not familiar with it. The Greek word *ekklēsia* that is translated as "church" in English Bibles was widely used for all sorts of assemblies. Call yourselves whatever makes sense. If you start a group and are looking for a nickname, feel free to use the title of this book, if that fits. I'd be honored. But while this title worked for a book on this subject, when it comes to a name for a group, you can surely do better. There are names I can think of that might be catchier that allude to popular TV series, such as *Extreme Faith Makeover* or *This Old Faith*. What title will seem appealing and who will find that it resonates with them are bound to differ dramatically. That's okay. It is a theme throughout this book that there is no one-size-fits-all approach.

Perhaps in an ideal world you could forgo labels. The earliest Christians were not called Christians. Today everyone except for fundamentalists tends to use a qualifier, from "Christian but not a fundamentalist" to "spiritual but not religious." Fundamentalism has never been the normative or dominant form of Christianity, and it should not be allowed to be viewed as the default today. A possible variety? Certainly. The most pure kind to which every other form is compared? By no means. God forbid! You may find labels like progressive, liberal, or open useful in the interest of avoiding confusion. It is not a new challenge to describe in a word or two who the followers of Jesus are and what we offer. I sometimes say that I want to call my variety of Christianity "critical Christianity" because it is committed to critical thinking and embraces the results of critical scholarship. Plus, the gatherings could then be called "critical mass." Alas, "critical" has as many negative connotations as "Christianity" does in at least some circles, and so I suspect that this punny name will not catch on. What about "Jesus Geeks"? It sounds just enough like "Jesus Freaks" to be a pun, without being the same phrase, and conveys what we might call "Jesus fandom." But just as some bristle at the label "Christian," others will resist being labeled a "geek."

As you can probably tell, I've stopped being completely serious at this point. What you call yourselves matters little, and you can always come up with a new name later. The movement that we refer to as Christians was around for some time before that actual label stuck, and was known by other names. What I do think is important is that you not cede a label that you really like just because it has been tarnished through its association with other individuals and groups. To be sure, religious labels are easier to swap than many others, such as national ones. If your national politics get embarrassing, you may hesitate before saying where you are from when traveling abroad. That's probably better than being proud in such circumstances. But you may then too want to emphasize that not all Americans are like that, just as many do in relation to Christianity. Being American (or British or Australian or anything else) has a longer and more diverse history than any one party or ideology represents. Whether you judge that history to be a mixed bag or mostly bad, our past doesn't entirely determine our future. Nations and people can change. That only happens when there is a movement to redefine what it means to be American, or British, or Christian, or evangelical, or whatever else. If there is a name that reflects your heritage, you have the option of working to reclaim it. You are under no obligation to give it up and replace it with something else.

As for the form your gatherings might take, pub theology is a model that some like. In other words, getting together somewhere relaxing where the music isn't so loud that it prevents conversation. That may be a great alternative to the traditional sermon and Sunday school class, or just a great venue for something not entirely unlike them, where those who've experienced church trauma won't be triggered by the surroundings. For communal singing, however, that venue won't be ideal (unless the proprietor is open to some unusual karaoke choices). Not everything you consider important needs to happen in the same place and at a single gathering. During the Communist era, Romanian Christians would meet for three hours on Sunday mornings because that was the only time the Communist authorities permitted them to gather in their church building. They packed sermon, prayer, Bible study, music, and lots more into that time. That made sense in that context. Today it is no longer required, and so most churches have shifted to multiple shorter gatherings with different aims. In the same way, individual components of typical services in churches in the English-speaking world may be separated, even if no church in your experience has ever done this.

Those gatherings don't even necessarily need to include all the same people. Just as, today, two individuals who go to the same church may never meet because they attend different services, perhaps with different styles of worship, it is fine to have different groups with which you pray, sing, study, feed the poor, advocate for changes in local and national policy, and whatever else you do as an expression of your faith. Instead of one congregation that is part of a denomination, the Christians of the future may be more like interconnected networks with points of overlap and interface. If that is less like the model of church that you are familiar with, it may be more akin to Paul's analogy with the body than he was aware of in his time, with his limited grasp of human anatomy. Our respiratory, circulatory, and digestive systems are distinguishable yet interconnected. As science progresses, it provides new analogies and models that we can draw on for a variety of purposes as Christians.

What about online community? While some consider it a pale substitute for "real" community, that hasn't been my experience. Once again my academic experience proves relevant. Teaching at a university with a small religious studies program, I do not have colleagues who are in the same field as me to read seminar papers to or bounce ideas off in person. In the age of blogging and social media, I found it didn't matter. I got to know scholars at other institutions, and we shared ideas and had conversations and debates electronically. When we met in person for the first time, it was like meeting an old friend. Online community can be real community. Now with Zoom and FaceTime, that is even more true.

Having said that, without *local* community involvement and connections there are things you won't be able to do. While hashtags have gone viral and supported grassroots movements, ultimately change happens when people are motivated to do something together in a specific place. Knowing that someone hundreds of miles away has your back is not the same as having someone literally stand alongside you. The fact that a thousand people in a Facebook forum agree with you will not sway a local library board not to give in to the pressure to remove books, whereas a mere dozen people showing up at the meeting in person might. Don't treat this as an either/or. Both are valuable. Sometimes the one can support or blend into the other.*

However much experience you had with fundamentalism, it was likely enough to convey the dangers of two opposite extremes in that tradition. One is the danger of excessive pressure to conform. The other is the danger of shutting oneself off from correction, insisting that "me and God make a majority." Think of how many people say that they have the Holy Spirit and the Bible and so they simply cannot be wrong. Think of how ironic it is that these individuals so often disagree with one another. Notice as well how clearly they have missed the implications of the conflict that arose between Paul and Peter in Antioch, about which the former wrote in his letter to the churches in the province of Galatia. If two apostles who had a personal encounter with Jesus can disagree, who am I to imagine that I cannot be wrong, that I have no need of correction? *Everyone* can be wrong, and I think I can safely say that everyone *will* be wrong sometimes. Here too I have learned something from academia. Each individual scholar tries out new ideas and explores new possibilities. Each of us can and will be wrong on our own, even if we are the leading expert on that particular subject. None of us is without biases. None of us sees everything clearly. The power of scholarly research is the interacting academic community that discusses, challenges, and confirms what any one of us concludes. We are stronger together. We see further together than any one of us can on our own. We expose and recognize bias

* For those in the field of education, we might want to explore ideas of hybrid church (like hybrid classes, blending in-person and online elements) and a flipped church model (like the flipped classroom, putting lectures/sermons online and using in-person meetings for activities that were previously considered homework).

together in ways we could not in isolation. Church at its best is like that as well.

It isn't just theological thinking that is at its best when connected to a network. While an individual can play a role in addressing societal injustice, ultimately they are only effective to the extent that others join in the effort.* Even music is better with multiple instruments. Not that there aren't lovely solo works, but ultimately few of us will be satisfied to only hear individual human voices sing and never a choir, or to only hear a solo violin but never with piano accompaniment or as part of a quartet. Nowadays it is possible to record music in ensemble without ever being in the same place. If you enjoy playing music, you will likely want to have the chance to play in person with other people at least from time to time, and perhaps as often as possible. The most important thing is that you get together to do the things that are important to you, and that you think carefully about exactly what is important to you as far as your faith is concerned.

I have emphasized throughout this book the need to define who you are, what you believe, and what your values are, and to do so in positive and not merely negative terms. The same applies to where you focus your conversations when you gather together. It may be helpful, if you have not yet had a chance to do so, to talk about your negative past experiences in a church context with others. Most who are reading this book have probably already done plenty of that. Recognize that some newcomers will likely still need an outlet for doing that. Also recognize the need to avoid having your community be characterized by gripefests. If and when you revisit unpleasant experiences, do so not to define yourself over

* Brian D. McLaren, *Do I Stay Christian? A Guide for the Doubters, the Disappointed, and the Disillusioned* (New York: St. Martin's, 2022), offers a compelling argument concerning the benefit of harnessing existing networks of people rather than trying to create much the same thing from scratch.

against the past in a negative way, but to work on being different in a positive way. Fundamentalist churches are regularly about how terrible life was before conversion and how terrible the world is, and thanking God for not being like that. That's one of the chief ways that so much that is toxic and profoundly unchristian manages to thrive in that religious tradition. Having previously been part of a group that insisted it was the good guys over against everyone else, I urge you not to repeat that mistake in what you are now working on creating. Fixating on complaining about others, seeing their faults rather than our own, is not the way of Jesus (Matt. 7:3–5; Luke 18:9–14). I mentioned that toward the beginning of the book, but like most important things, it bears repeating as we now reach the end. Define yourself, but not too rigidly, in a manner that welcomes rather than excludes. Define your identity as a unifying core rather than with boundary walls. Define your identity in terms of who you are and what you stand for, rather than what you are not and what you are against.

Conclusion

As this book draws to a close, let me offer one last suggestion about finding or making community that works, explores, experiences, and connects. Just talk to people. More than anything else, that seems to be how Christianity spread at the very beginning. Don't know what to talk about? Let me help. Talk about this book. If someone seems genuinely interested, lend it to them or buy them a copy. As happy as selling more copies makes an author, that isn't my aim in recommending this. I myself am an introvert and a Christian who has sometimes wondered whether anyone else was wrestling with the things I am. Often a book I was reading was a way to start a conversation, just as sometimes the author describing their own experience showed that they too were exploring the things that I was. If the person you are talking to reacts negatively to the book, the author can take the flak. If the other person can relate, the words of the author can provide the bridge and open a door to further conversation.

When I say "just talk to people," I know how difficult that is, for some readers more than others. As an introvert who decided to become an educator, I have had to become used to going into a room full of strangers and being the one to get things started. A hint of nervousness is always there, and that's okay. Things that are worth doing are usually risky. Do them anyway. But don't be afraid to get help. It is available, at least from afar but probably from closer than you think. If my book can help get a conversation, or a reading group, or a Sunday school series started that helps those reconstructing their faith do so, I will be glad. I hope that at some point, in a letter or email or blog comment, you'll let me know.

That's for later. For now, just take stock of where you are. You may already be further along in identifying a solid foundation and framing a new structure on top of it than you were when you first set eyes on page 1. Keep going. Don't give up. Build a worldview, build habits, build friendships. Share your faith in its new form. Share your story. It is still every bit as worthy of being called your *testimony* as what you might have said in years or decades past. You are on a journey, and your story will be ongoing. The way you tell and share it may change more than once in the future. Don't wait until it seems "settled" before making further changes. And don't wait until it seems "settled" before telling me about it. If this book offered you any encouragement, hearing about how it did so will encourage me. Whatever local and online communities you join or create, we are part of a larger whole, a bigger and even more diverse movement. I shared my story hoping it would be helpful to you. What should you do now? Move beyond deconstruction, craft a better faith than the one you left behind, find ways to articulate your worldview in positive terms, and pay the favor forward, sharing your story with others who will in turn do likewise, on and on, so that together we build something greater and more beautiful than any of us could alone, in Jesus's name, and to the glory of God.

Key Points from This Chapter

- Include other human conversation partners as you explore the process of positive worldview construction and theologizing.
- The need for community is a human one and not merely a religious one.
- Church did not originally involve sitting in pews and listening to one person speak from the front. Explore other models and possibilities for community, ones that make room for conversation.
- There may be existing communities that you could meaningfully become part of, but creating a new one is also an option.
- Even if it was not your past experience, it is possible for a community to uphold all its members while respecting the different journeys they are on and stages they are at.
- Local connection is important, not only for one's mental and spiritual well-being but also when it comes to working for societal change.
- There needs to be room for complaint, but it is important to not only fixate on what has been or continues to be wrong. Find ways to turn criticism into positive mental and social effort to be and do better.

For Reflection and Discussion

Reflect on a time when you have felt lonely on your spiritual path. What would have been valuable to you at that time? Where might you find that now, and how can you find opportunities to meet the need of others in their similar moments?

Who have you talked with about your religious journey? Is there someone with whom you wish you could talk but have not had the courage to? Can sharing or talking about this book open a door and help start a conversation?

Where have you found meaningful connections, even if they have not included discussion of religion or worldview? Could room be made there for conversations about your convictions and exploration, and those of others?

Think about beliefs and practices that you discarded as you became disillusioned with the faith you once had. Were any of them discarded too hastily? Might they or something like them, even if an adapted form or interpreted in a new way, have the potential to play a positive role where you are now and where you see yourself headed?

Humans use language to label things and convey meaning to others. What words seem apt for explaining your worldview to others in positive terms? Why those words?

Now that you have reached the end of this book, which of the chapters stands out most prominently in your mind? Which did you find most meaningful and why? What do you intend to do to explore that aspect of your life of faith?